THE ILLUSTRATED MANUAL OF
SNIPER SKILLS

THE ILLUSTRATED MANUAL OF
SNIPER SKILLS

MARK SPICER

ZENITH PRESS

First published in 2006 by Zenith Press, an imprint of MBI Publishing Company, 400 First Avenue North, Minneapolis, MN 55401 USA

MBI Publishing Company titles are also available at discounts in bulk quantity for industrial or sales-promotional use. For details write to Special Sales Manager at MBI Publishing Company, 400 First Avenue North, Minneapolis, MN 55401 USA

Project manager: Ray Bonds
Design: Ian Hughes/Compendium Design
Editors: Ray Bonds and Don Gulbrandsen
Diagrams: Mark Franklin and Stephen Spicer

ISBN-13: 978-0-7603-2674-9
ISBN-10: 0-7603-2674-6

Printed in China

Author's Acknowledgments

I would like to thank the following for their help and support: my wife Diane, daughter Gemma, and son Stephen; Harry Tyman; the snipers of 1 PWRR for proving my training ethos in combat; Syd Hawkins; Jim Dowle; Neil & Elizabeth Morris; and all snipers still risking their lives around the world.

Additional photographs

Front cover: A corporal with the sniper platoon of the 1st Battalion, the Princess of Wales's Royal Regiment, fires an Accuracy International .50-caliber rifle at insurgents attacking a British camp in Al Amara, Iraq.

Back cover: (top left) a sniper's target seen at distance through a telescopic sight; (bottom left) German Army snipers blend into their surroundings during mountain training; (right) a sniper takes aim, camouflaged so as to merge into the background of a bombed-out building in an urban environment.

Page 1: A sniper uses natural foliage as camouflage to help fool thermal imagers.

Pages 2-3: A sniper team operating in Iraq, July 2004.

Pages 4-5: A sniper and his observer during training on the mountainous German/Austrian border.

Pages 6-7: A sniper pair demonstrating the effectiveness of an anti-thermal camouflage suit.

CONTENTS

INTRODUCTION

The ability of snipers—single men or women, or a pair or group, be they police or military—to inflict severe and far-reaching damage to individuals, or a small or large formation of people, or equipment, or area, is well proven. Some people will feel that this subject is taboo and has no business being written about. But recent world events show that those who would use this type of tactic to inflict damage and hurt upon the innocent are already doing so, and have been for some time. Sniping—because it is simple to use, easy to maintain, and cheap to produce—has not gone unnoticed by the lower levels of human society. Indeed, evidence shows that those inclined to use it as a means of terror against the innocent seem to have a much better grasp of its uses than do many military and police forces.

It is clear that in certain areas the hierarchy either fail to fully understand the many and diverse uses of the sniper, or they choose to ignore them in the hope that nobody ever uses snipers against their own forces. Of course, the task of balancing a budget with plans to protect a country and its population is not an easy one. Certainly, knowledgeable people from any area of defense could provide plausible arguments for investment in many other pieces of equipment and training, and in any event unless snipers are integrated into a layered system they will fail, as alone they are not the answer. However, for a small force taking on a much larger and more powerful one, attrition becomes the tactic and sniping becomes a viable option.

About now many people may be claiming that I have just given the thumbs-up to any lunatic or terrorist who wishes to cause mayhem and murder. However, the

LEFT: Armor has always been considered to be unaffected by small arms fire, but knowledge of the machine and its equipment makes it vulnerable. Today's tanks are reliant upon computers and optics, and to a sniper these all become legitimate targets.

lunatic and the terrorist have already embraced the benefits of sniping, and for many years have been utilizing this tactic to a much larger and better degree than many of the major military powers have done.

We can either ignore what the terrorists already know, and hope they don't get any smarter, or we can expand on the subject to ensure that weak areas in our own knowledge, and therefore our defenses, are closed, by using literature to ensure our own forces have access to knowledge that should be, but is not easily, available. Knowledge is strength, and to understand how a skill or tactic can be used against you is to have the knowledge to defend against it.

BELOW: A British sniper of the 1st Battalion, the Princess of Wales's Royal Regiment, takes aim at insurgents attacking a British outpost in Iraq. He has both a night optical sight and back-up assault rifle at hand, indicating the level of combat the unit encountered.

In my travels around the world and during my time in the armed forces I have been privileged to come into contact with many very dedicated and professional men and women (although I have never encountered a female sniper within the military, unlike their colleagues in the law enforcement community who have recognized the abilities of females in this skill). From these professionals I have learned as much as I have ever taught. Most of this knowledge, gained either from personal experience or from the experience of others they have encountered, has been transferred by word of mouth. The basic fact that all this knowledge should have been recorded and invested in the training of the next generation of snipers is obvious. Because this has not been done, this book is aimed at helping them to understand and to expand their knowledge of sniping skills. It covers the basic sniper skills, shooting techniques, shot placement, operating in varying environments (from, for instance, urban

ABOVE: German mountain troops practice engaging targets high up in the mountains above them. These soldiers are among the best mountain troops in the world and the snipers are trained to a very high standard.

BELOW LEFT: A British sniper in Iraq utilizing the shadow and depth of a room to provide a concealed urban shooting position into the street outside. Notice how he has improvised a shooting platform from the furniture and is shooting through a small opening to maximize his ability to remain unseen.

BELOW RIGHT: Wearing an improvised rock camouflage smock, a German sniper maximizes his concealment against the rock he is using to elevate his rifle to engage targets higher up the mountain.

scenarios to desert conditions), counter-sniping, and sniper weapons. The aim has been two-fold: to provide extra knowledge for the sniper to add to his or her personal arsenal of options, and to provide potential targets of the terrorist sniper with knowledge with which to protect themselves or others under their care.

One of the main aspects of sniping about which there appears a true lack of under-standing is that of counter-sniping. Many units across the spectrum of sniper-capable forces deploy or at least claim to deploy a counter-sniper option. To many the old and accurate cry of "the best way to remove a

sniper is with another sniper" is the limit of their counter-sniper thought process. After all, if you encounter a sniper who is causing damage to, or the delaying of, your forces, he has to be removed.

Today's world is one where all-out war and the lack of thought for or concern towards civilian welfare or property are highly unlikely, and so heavy indirect fire or close air support against enemy snipers are not viable options. Those who say the use of smart technology means you can accurately bomb a sniper in an urbanized area nowadays have missed the point that even the concrete-only bombs that use kinetic energy rather than explosive warheads to accomplish their task still create large amounts of collateral damage to both property and people. Therefore, the best counter-sniper option would appear to be to deploy your own sniper.

ABOVE: A British sniper with an improvised urban camouflage suit and a shooting tripod made from a camera tripod takes up position in the rubble of derelict buildings. The suit and the shadow he has used make him very difficult to locate.

In my view this is a final resort; the true counter-sniper option is to have used tactics and drills that severely restrict if not negate the ability of your enemy to deploy snipers against you in the first place. Here, surely, is the true meaning of the counter-sniper option. The only way to encompass this skill is to identify and foster the experience and knowledge of those within your forces, collating sniper experience into a central pool and ensuring it is disseminated back down to those who need it, trusting in the judgment of those selected to interpret the intelligence.

Today the sniper may well have a variety

of weapons, ammunition calibers, and ammunition natures to choose from, depending on the type of target and the capabilities of his opponent. Manufacturers endeavor to invent ammunition to cover all eventualities, and then to invent defenses against that ammunition, leading on to a new cycle of ammunition invention. While this may be great for global economy, it presents the sniper with a never-ending list of targets, as his ammunition becomes more effective against more equipment and reaches further and with greater consistency against human targets.

Within the world of the Special Forces soldier this increased list of target options is backed up with a teaching of shot placement aimed to achieve maximum damage at the target end. The same cannot be said, I fear, for the lowly infantry or marine sniper. Indeed, I have never seen a lesson plan on shot placement for equipment targets. The effects of any caliber ammunition on today's high technology equipment are glossed over

ABOVE: Airfields are very vulnerable to sniper fire, since aircraft are easy to disable. This airfield is under sniper observation from a concealed OP position and its activity is being relayed back to the snipers' command. Snipers use their ability to hide and observe as much as they do their ability to shoot.

or ignored completely. Pilots of all aircraft, especially helicopters, are well aware of the repercussions of well or luckily placed small arms fire. But the pilot is not the only one to have reason to fear small arms fire, as there are many military and civilian machines that do not react too well to the adding of high-speed lead to their working parts; while it may not destroy an object, well placed small arms fire will reduce operational effectiveness and either remove it from use for a period of time, or render it vulnerable to other attacks.

The knowledge of how to attack, and where the vulnerabilities in the equipment's systems are will always lead to the ability to identify and better protect weak areas. Part of the role of the true counter-sniper team is to encompass identification of potential attack and the consequences of such an attack, and to aid in risk assessment and therefore development of a counter-plan to stop such an attack becoming a reality. Awareness of actual damaged caused by, or the potential damage from, correct shot placement will inevitably highlight areas of weakness or of concern, and will allow the defensive sniper team to increase protective measures accordingly.

The key to maximizing damage to equipment is in knowing how it works. This does not mean that the sniper must have a degree in electronics or be able to fly an aircraft; it merely means that he should have a basic working knowledge of various types of technology, just as he is taught to recognize aircraft and vehicles. This extra knowledge can easily be gained by taking any opportunity to speak to the men and women in their own forces who operate this equipment, or by asking innocent questions at foreign air shows, for instance, and other technology displays, and playing up to the human need to feel important! It is amazing how much information the average person

BELOW: Many airfields are overlooked by high ground on at least one of their sides. With the proliferation of .50-caliber weapons, and the sniper's ability to shoot over long ranges, airfields are under a greater threat than ever before.

will give to grab a moment of false superiority over another—and all you have to do is ask stupid questions! As an alternative, there are hosts of available books, periodicals, and films that cover the subject, or a sniper may be able to produce his own.

It is worth highlighting the need for the infantry sniper to pay attention to naval forces as well as the threats posed by aircraft and land vehicles. This might elicit the

ABOVE: A British sniper takes aim with an Accuracy International AW50 .50-caliber sniper rifle in southern Iraq. The .50-caliber gives the sniper a vastly greater range than the standard 7.62mm/.308-caliber sniper rifles.

sarcastic retort, "Well, you always come across frigates in the middle of a tank battle!" But the simple fact is that today you never know when you will be called upon to attack or defend any one of a wide range of targets, including naval facilities, ships, aircraft, or indeed industrial property; after all, the Iraq conflict has seen troops deployed in port facilities, rivers, oil fields, and cities, first attacking, and now having to protect, the entire infrastructure of a country.

Sniper skills identified and perfected over many years and through many conflicts remain effective today and should still form the foundation of all basic sniper training. The standards set and maintained by our forbears have been proved to work many times over the years. The emergence of ever more astonishing technology will have an effect on how and where the sniper can be effective, but it does not mean he is out of date. Abandoning tried and tested methods and standards of concealment, movement, and tactics is not called for and only leads to a less effective and therefore less employable asset. While not all snipers could or should be trained the same way, there is a very good argument for a basic minimum of standards that enable the end product to expand or become flexible enough to be deployed in all scenarios.

Operational commitments, the availability of suitable manpower, the time it takes to train snipers, and budgetary restrictions all combine to make the production of a sniper cadre, fully trained to deploy worldwide, a very difficult prospect indeed. But this difficulty should not be allowed to consign this age-old skill to the trashcan or mediocrity.

The establishment and maintenance of Special Forces are even more demanding, but still occur. The sniper is not seen as an SF soldier, but he is a specialist and has the ability to seriously contribute to a variety of military, police, and civil defense options, in addition to his obvious attack potential— and he is very cheap. The selection process and attributes of the sniper are in keeping with those associated with the SF soldier. With an operational doctrine based on small unit deployments, domination of much larger forces, severe risk of capture, and fighting against the odds, the sniper would have claim to being a special type of force. As commanders start to re-learn the value of these men, we shall see a more extensive use

of the sniper's skills and abilities in all operational deployments around the world's current hot-spots. Some snipers have indeed been used on SF operations; and while many snipers would not pass SF selection, many SF operators would not pass a sniper course.

In the "green army" world, sniping is a very demanding skill and much more so than in the often quoted "black army" sniper one. The line between the two is now often blurred; any role that the SF operator carries out is often regarded as that of a "black" operation, which used to concern anti-terrorist direct action roles, where highly trained SF marksmen provide eyes and ears for the assault force, and protective fire; it now covers any operation deemed covert, and is as much a design of self-survival by the SF world as an actual type of operation. The selection process of correctly trained snipers, and the attributes required to pass and then be deployed operationally, are just as specialized and should be recognized as such. With the role of the Special Forces becoming wider in the war against terror, they find themselves stretched more thinly on the ground, a situation exacerbated by increasing numbers leaving the forces to take up well-paid jobs in private security. It would therefore appear to make sense to recognize and utilize the skill and determination of the sniper to assist in the surveillance and reconnaissance areas of this combat arena.

Some countries are indeed looking at making their sniper force a divisional one, with command and control kept at the highest level alongside their Special Forces, and deploying them in support of all levels of operations. This will only ever work if the countries concerned dedicate time and money to ensuring the correct level of selection, training, and control of these forces. Only this will allow for the trust and belief to be built up in military and law enforcement commanders to a level where they will consider sniper deployment as a viable option alongside all other assets.

In this book I aim to illustrate the value of keeping old levels of training and enhancing them, not replacing them, with newer and just as relevant skills, thereby producing an ever expanding option for armed forces and law enforcement commanders, rather than a new one. Never throw away an old skill since you never know when you may need it. Snipers are not just men who shoot well; they are excellent infantry soldiers who also have the ability and skill to carry out specialized sniper operations as a unit or as a pair. This level of skill and professionalism is wasted unless recognized and restructured to maximize its effect.

LEFT: High up in the Alps three German snipers survey the mountain passes below them while remaining concealed. The effect of the improvised "rock" camouflage smock is evident, with the man on the left blending into the rock to his rear. From hundreds of feet below these snipers would be almost impossible to locate.

BELOW: Snipers deploy onto a high Alpine mountain pass to provide overwatch and a defensive perimeter. Snipers would prove very difficult to detect and remove in this type of terrain.

CHAPTER 1 TRAINING THE SNIPER

There is a widespread misconception as to exactly what constitutes sniping. Many people seem to believe it is the ability to shoot accurately over very long distances. But this is simply not the case; the ability to shoot accurately over long ranges is by no means the sole prerogative of the sniper. Indeed, any number of civilian hunting and shooting clubs have as members people with an admirable ability to hit targets up to and past the one thousand yards mark, but they are by no means trained snipers. Sniping is a tactical skill, which is not related to range or distance. The ability to utilize that tactic over long ranges is a useful by-product of being able to shoot well, but is by no means a prerequisite of employing sniping tactics.

Sniping is the employment of individual shooters from concealed positions with no warning, from any distance, depending on the range of the weapon This is not to say, of course, that to maximize the chances of the sniper surviving to fight again, the longer the distance between him and the victim the better. Conversely, if the sniper is able to conceal himself and engage successfully at close range, then that is also sniping. The corollary is, of course, that someone under sniper fire should not fall into the trap of looking into the distance every time a shot is heard; the shooter may be right under his nose, just relying on his intended victim's pre-

ABOVE: The sniper has selected a position that provides him with a screening bush in front of him and the bank behind to provide a backdrop in which to disappear. This, combined with shadow, would make him difficult to locate by an enemy under attack from him.

conceived idea that he will be further away.

Sniping is a combination of several skills of which shooting is certainly among the most important, although it is in many ways the easiest to teach and learn, and for this reason it is usually the first phase of most sniper courses. If trainees cannot shoot with consistency, there is no point in wasting time and resources trying to get them through other skills.

The precise definition of a sniper and sniping will vary, but the British Army definition forms a useful and generally accepted starting point:

"The sniper is a selected soldier who is a trained marksman and observer, who can locate and report on an enemy, however well concealed, who can stalk or lie in wait unseen, and kill with one shot."

Sniper selection and training

Successful sniper units are usually a product of the correct selection process and continuation training. The individuals in these units are usually quiet professionals who go about their business with little or no supervision, and who are happy with their own company and yet are still capable of being a part of a professional and supportive team. They are consistent shots, are above average in all basic

ABOVE: This sniper has done well to conceal himself, but has allowed the "Butler creek" type lens cover to protrude from his camouflage, where its black circular shape will give him away.

skills, including fitness, and display a maturity and tendency for humor. The qualities that should be looked for when recruiting for or creating a sniper unit may well vary from one army or unit to the next, and will be influenced by a country's religion, attitudes towards soldiering, past experiences of sniping, size of the available pool of talent, and mental attributes of the nation's men and women. In general, however, most armies would look for the following attributes in potential candidates.

- Military skills: above average.
- Marksmanship: outstanding or with the potential to achieve it.

- Intelligence: vital for the sniper, who will have to able to read a tactical situation and assess the consequences of his actions.
- Maturity and mental fitness: of importance to the sniper, who must be aware of his responsibilities and be prepared to accept them.
- Physical fitness: essential for a sniper, but bearing in mind that he is not so much a sprinter as a long-distance runner who must be able to work for protracted periods.
- Sense of humor: essential for snipers, whose lives are often harsh and unforgiving.
- Non-smoker: this may seem out of place, but the chances of a sniper being in a safe enough area to light a cigarette during operations are always slim, and someone who is yearning to smoke will not be fully alert.

Following from these attributes, the potential sniper needs seven primary skills that must be developed and mastered in order to become a qualified sniper:
- Shooting
- Observation
- Judging distance
- Navigation
- Sniper-related knowledge
- Camouflage and concealment
- Stalking

The standards are and must remain harsh, in the same manner as those for Special Forces, since the life and stress of

BELOW: A British sniper instructor oversees joint training with French Foreign Legion and Belgian Para Commandos in Kosovo. Cross training with other units is essential in today's multinational task force deployments.

ABOVE: While out of sight of his enemy, this sniper has made the fatal mistake of allowing himself to become the focus of entertainment for a cow. Its size and curiosity will draw attention to this area, and hence to the sniper.

being an operational sniper is such that to lower standards in order to satisfy a pass quota is to risk lives unnecessarily. The standards and teaching methods employed on basic sniper courses should remain very similar to those that were taught at the first sniper schools in World War I—teaching and training should be for the worst-case scenario, and there is nothing worse than what those men had to face! This training ethos is essential because, while the sniper's equipment has changed considerably over the years, the role of the sniper has not.

Shooting. When selecting personnel to attend a basic sniper course an aptitude for shooting must be present; ideally, potential trainees have already achieved marksman status. Military students will have been trained in the recognized shooting positions and have achieved a level of experience using the standard issue infantry rifles. However, the law-enforcement candidate may never have used a long gun, and so this part of training will naturally take up more time on a police course than it will on a military one. The candidates will then follow a structured program of instruction that will cover weapon-handling, shooting techniques, shooting positions, and ballistics, culminating in a sniper qualification shoot.

Marksmanship principles

- The position and hold must be firm enough to support the weapon.
- The weapon must point naturally at the target without any undue effort.
- The sight alignment must be correct.
- The shot must be released and followed through without disturbance to the position.

ABOVE: A British sniper in observing training using the very reliable Leica Vector laser rangefinder binoculars. To his right is the Leopold x40 spotting scope issued to British and several other army snipers.

Observation. The sniper must have the ability to locate an enemy, no matter how well concealed, and so must have a natural curiosity to investigate and question. Most people live in an urban environment, and they seldom look at objects that are greater than a few hundred yards away. The sniper, especially the law-enforcement officer who lives and works mainly in this environment, must train at distance and in detail. Observation is about locating the enemy, and gathering information or intelligence. This has to include the penetration of camouflage, natural and false.

The sniper will depend on his eyesight to gather intelligence after locating the enemy, and also to ensure his own safety, and so must not only have a keen sense of sight but must also be proficient in the use of any optical aids that may be available to him. He must therefore be trained in the correct use and maintenance of such items as binoculars,

BELOW: A British sniper moves cautiously forward towards an overwatch OP position in Northern Ireland. In that trouble-torn province snipers often used their ability to move unseen to occupy positions from which to observe and report on terrorist activity.

telescopes, and night-vision equipment.

Before a sniper can be effective in the use of optical aids, he must first master the proper use of his eyes, which is achieved through a combination of physical effort and mental attitude. The physical side of the training takes the form of observing over long distances under operational-type conditions and is a progressive series of exercises, but this training is preceded by mental alertness education, since people can often see something only when they are aware that it is out of the ordinary.

Methods of observation

Hasty search. The hasty search is a swift check of an area for any signs of enemy activity, which should take no longer than approximately thirty seconds. First, the sniper will carry out a check of all the prominent areas within his arc of responsibil-

ity, ensuring he works right to left or left to right in a systematic pattern to achieve total coverage and avoid missing any point. While the search is systematic it is not sweeping, being a rapid check of specific points. The reason for this is that when the eye is focused onto one specific point, its peripheral vision will detect movement over a wide area around that specific point, thus alerting the sniper to any activity that might represent a potential threat to his life.

Detailed search. The sniper now carries out a thorough search of the area, again using a systematic breakdown of the arc of responsibility, with each area being checked in detail

BELOW: A sniper pair move forward through wooded terrain to occupy a shooting position against their intended target. The weather never stops operations, and so snipers must be able to operate under all conditions.

before moving on to the next. The sniper will start at either the far right or far left of his arc and move across to the opposite side, breaking the ground down into left, center, and right, and search each to a depth of approximately fifty yards. The search will begin with the ground closest to the sniper, as this is the area that presents the highest risk to him should the enemy make an appearance, giving the sniper less time to react. Each third—left, center, or right—will then be broken down into near, middle, and distance. Once the near areas have been checked the sniper will move on to the middle ground, that being the next area of highest risk, and then on to the distant areas to complete the search. Each distance should cover left, middle, and right to ensure that the entire arc is scrutinized, and each area should be overlapped by about ten yards to make sure that nothing is accidentally missed.

Assuming that the sniper is working as a pair with an observer, after the search has been completed the sniper pair must keep a check on the area and monitor any areas of interest using the hasty search method. They will also need to carry out a detailed search at irregular intervals to ensure that nothing has changed; if it has, then they must use their powers of observation and deduction to find out why. The use of any optic will, over a fairly short period of time, produce eyestrain or fatigue, and the sniper pair will start to miss things without even realizing, due to reduced effectiveness of the eye's performance. For this reason it is essential that the observation be spread evenly between the sniper and the observer, reducing the chance of missing anything, and improving the pair's security.

Observation at night. The sniper pair must be as observant and cautious at night as they are during the day. The eye uses a different part of its make-up at night compared to that during daylight; whereas daylight uses the center part of the eye, at night the outer part of the pupil is most effective. For this reason

BELOW: These snipers have taken the easy and direct route across a field instead of scouting the edges and remaining unseen, which would have been harder and taken longer, but would have kept them concealed from the enemy. Being lazy could easily be being dead!

BELOW: This sniper pair is making the most of the trapped shadow the building offers, in conjunction with the bushes. However, caution must be shown, since the sun moves, and hence so will the shadow!

the "off-center" vision method is employed by snipers at night. This is achieved by looking at about four to six inches off-center of the object to be viewed, and in this way a true image of the object's shape will come into focus. This is because if a human looks directly at an object at night, the image will blur and lose definition, due to the inner part of the pupil's lack of clarity in darkness.

Range estimation. The ability to assess the range between the observer and the object being observed is very important. Even with the abundance of range-finding equipment available, there will always be a need to judge range without technological aids. The sniper must be aware of this, and during his training several different methods to judge distance without the aid of expensive lasers should be taught. There are only two main methods of judging distance.

The first of these, the appearance

ABOVE: There is nothing in nature that is black! This sniper's black binoculars highlight his position and make his camouflage a waste of time. Lack of attention to detail can get you killed.

method, depends on the sniper's ability to retain information or, to be more specific, an image. The way it works is to stand a soldier in all his fighting equipment about a hundred yards away from the troops being trained. The troops then observe the soldier by the naked eye and with any optics available to them as a part of their normal operational kit. They then make a mental note of exactly how much detail they can see on the soldier at the hundred yards distance: for example, all his equipment can be seen in detail, his skin tone is visible, and his limbs and extremities can be easily picked out. The soldier is moved back to about two hundred yards, and the process is repeated, continuing out to about six hundred yards, where the detail that could previously be seen is now lost, and just the general outline of the soldier can be seen. Notes on the detail that could be seen at each given range should be completed for reference for later use.

Appearance method guide

200 yards—clear in all detail, color, skin tone, equipment.
300 yards—clear body outline, face color good, face detail blurred.
400 yards—clear body outline, all other detail blurred.
500 yards—body begins to taper with head less distinctive.
600 yards—body appears wedge-shaped, no head apparent.

In the unit-of-measure method the sniper trainee mentally pictures a known distance and then compares it to the distance between him and the target. For example, using the length of a football field as the known distance, the sniper will visualize how many football fields will fit into the distance to be judged; if the target is four field-lengths away the total distance is about four hundred to four hundred forty yards. This system, as with others, will require practice and has two limitations:

• It only works up to four hundred yards.
• It is not effective over dead ground.

When judging distance it is also important to know that objects will seem closer or farther away under certain conditions, as shown in the accompanying box.

Factors making objects seem closer

The object (for example, an armored vehicle) is larger than other objects in its immediate vicinity.
There is dead ground between the object and the observer.
The object is higher than the observer (who is therefore looking up).
Light shining onto the nearside of the object (making the detail clearer).

Factors making objects seem farther away

The object is smaller than other objects in its vicinity.
The sunlight is bright or dazzling the observer.
The observer is looking down (down a street, a forest ride, etc.).
The observer is lying down.

Optical aids to judging distance. The most reliable and most frequently used method of range estimation for the sniper is the reticule pattern within his scope or spotting scope. The reticule can be used to accurately measure the target distance, as long as the object's height is known. This is due to the reticule being in millimeters (mils), one mil subtending to one meter at a thousand meters, and so the range can be estimated with a fair degree of accuracy. This method is effective over dead ground or when there are differences in height between the target and the sniper. The target needs to be accurately measured, so the optic should be rested on a

ABOVE: Today's snipers have all manner of optical devices to assist them in locating and identifying their prey. Modern telescopic sights have very good clarity of vision and high-power zoom magnification. To underestimate or discount snipers is to invite death. With a sniper team or teams deployed, standing out on this balcony could prove to be fatal!

stable base, preferably a purpose-built tripod. Too high an estimation will produce better results than too low, although an accuracy of 0.25 mils is recommended when measuring. The whole process works off a commonly used formula and has proved to be an adequate way of range estimation. The equation is as follows:

$$\frac{\text{Known height of target x 1,000}}{\text{Reticle measurement in mils}} = \text{range (in meters)}$$

$$\text{For example: } \frac{4 \times 1000}{4} = 1,000\text{m}$$

Navigation

The ability to navigate his way across different types of terrain is very important to any soldier, but is of exceptional importance to the sniper and sniper team. Such teams will often be traveling concealed and be in positions where standing up and looking around is just not a viable option, usually due to proximity to the enemy or a hostile population. For this reason it is vital that snipers learn how to navigate to a high standard and can identify their exact position under all types of conditions and in all types of terrain.

Camouflage and concealment

This is a fundamental skill of the sniper, where his ability to remain unseen is essential to survival, and one where very successful, if somewhat difficult, training methods exist and have changed little since the sniper training of World War I. Efforts to lower the difficulty levels in such skills to satisfy the "pass quota" norms almost invariably result in a drop in standards, leading to a sniper who is simply not adequately equipped for his job and a danger both to himself and to his comrades. The sniper recruit must learn to conceal himself in different types of terrain and flora, and in varying periods of time. The reason for the time restriction is to

ABOVE: The skill in camouflage is to be able to read the weather and the conditions around you. This sniper has utilized the color of his ghillie suit to move across a similarly colored field with minimum risk of detection.

BELOW: By using dead ground and the screening effect of the foliage along the road's edge, this sniper is able to pass by the civilian community at work around him and occupy an observation position further down the road.

ABOVE: Another sniper who, through lack of attention to detail, has given himself away to the enemy. His black boots draw the eye, and once they are found, so is he, since badgers have yet to discover high leg boots!

BELOW: Snipers must be very aware of the basics of survival, since they often operate behind the enemy lines or in very forward positions. This basic shelter would serve a sniper pair well if deep in a wooded area in harsh weather.

enable him to learn to identify and occupy positions of concealment rapidly in order to protect himself from approaching danger, whether from enemy soldiers or civilian population, and therefore remain unseen and safe. The sniper should also receive training and education in all manner of camouflage techniques and scenarios, from rural through to urban, which will enable him to be deployed with minimal notice into any operational theater.

Stalking

Without doubt the primary skill associated with the sniper is stalking, encompassing all other skills within it. Failure to master one of the other skills will lead to an inability to master the stalk. The sniper will always be outnumbered and outgunned by his adversary, and so to remain unseen and able to maneuver into a position of advantage is a very high priority. The ability to study available maps and pictures, and to assess routes and levels of difficulty, and then to modify the selected route during the actual operation, take time and patience to learn and master. Not only does the sniper have to be able to move through heavy foliage, but he must also learn how to camouflage himself and move unseen in all manner of terrains, and this particular skill is one that requires constant practice.

BELOW: A sniper will live longer if he is aware of his surroundings and does not cut corners. This sniper advances across an open field but has the sense to use the shadow and hedgerow to screen his movement.

BELOW: Lack of thought could get you killed. In one unguarded moment this sniper has exposed his otherwise concealed location by getting a white map out (center of photo) without shielding it from view.

ABOVE AND BELOW: Snipers have to be able to identify ground that will prove advantageous to them. Here a sniper pair have to cross an open field, in which they would normally be vulnerable, so they reduce their profile by traversing it using tank or tractor tracks already in the field.

Sniper-associated skills

This is a somewhat blanket requirement that encompasses all the other associated skills that a sniper team must add to their knowledge in order for them to become versatile, deployable assets. This covers such areas as foreign weapon recognition and handling, equipment and vehicle recognition, and, for the purpose of anti-materiel operations, should also include ship, aircraft, and civilian equipment recognition. The natural follow-on to this type of training is the expansion of the sniper's shooting skills with different weapons, such as the .338- and .50-caliber sniper weapons, and their tactical deployment options. Other skills like nuclear, biological and chemical (NBC) warfare and how it affects sniper operations, will have to be learned, as will sniper operations in different terrains, such as deserts and mountains, especially now that deployments to areas like Iraq and Afghanistan are becoming more frequent.

ABOVE: Many units neglect essential skills during training and assume they will still retain an overall skill level. This is wrong, since most sniper skills are perishable and so should be programmed in to maintain a skill base. Here the author maintains his pistol skills during training.

BELOW: Snipers train to use an improvised shooting tripod fashioned from cut wood and then camouflaged. Good snipers are masters of using what they find around them.

Shooting

The sniper has to be able to shoot from any recognized position and some he will have to invent on the spot in order to make a particular shot, so it follows that the sniper and the instructor must spend time training to shoot in as many positions as seem feasible. It is claimed by traditional shooting teachers that to deviate from the recognized positions leads to poor results, but the sniper is taught that as long as he applies the four basic marksmanship principles, and at the moment of shot release the cross hairs are on the target, he will hit home, no matter how awkward the position may look.

The trainee selected to attend a basic sniper course should have shown an aptitude for shooting and ideally have achieved the unit's marksman status. This is not always the case and the joining standard is not always met, leaving both instructors and students struggling to achieve a standard, often against the clock. This is the main reason many students fail at an early stage, which is not always their fault, but because

BELOW: A view of the zeroing range in the Austrian Army mountain barracks used by a German mountain sniper course. The author was privileged to attend this course in 2002 during a break from a tour in Kosovo.

they have been wrongly put forward for the sniper course by a platoon commander or SWAT captain, who probably does not understand the standards required and was reluctant to ask for fear of appearing stupid.

All basic students will already have been trained in the recognized shooting positions and have a basic level of shooting experience using their own army's or police force's standard issue rifle. The sniper students then go through a course of instruction covering weapon handling, shooting techniques, shooting positions, and ballistics, culminating in the sniper qualification shoot.

Safe weapon handling

Every sniper student must be fully conversant with the weapon of his or her unit's choice and must be able to deploy and move around with it day-to-day in a safe manner. This will be the first time that many students have worked with a bolt-action or adjustable-

ABOVE: A sniper uses his ghillie suit and natural local foliage to conceal himself from view while observing enemy forces. His partner, who is out of sight, provides mutual support while the sniper reports on the enemy's movements.

triggered rifle. The students will be taught the weapon from the basics upwards, covering not only safe handling but also such areas as stripping and assembly, load and unload, the telescopic sight, and the use of the rifle sling. They will then be taught how to zero their own personal weapon and how to adjust it to fit them to make the rifle their own, although they will also be taught how to compensate for the use of a weapon that is set up for someone else, such as their partner.

The snipers will be taught the smooth operation of the weapon's bolt and to avoid rapid arm movements when chambering a round, unless engaging multiple targets and using the rapid bolt manipulation technique,

ABOVE: The author checking the zero of an Accuracy International sniper rifle during a German Army mountain sniper course. The German Army selected the weapon (designated G22 in German service) as its standard sniper rifle, as did the British Army and many others.

which will also be taught. It will be explained to the students that the bolt-action rifle is still the preferred choice of most professional snipers, since the bolt gun is easier to control. It is, therefore, quicker to re-acquire any secondary targets when compared to the semi-automatic rifle, although it has to be said that several semi-automatic rifles are now of a comparable accuracy to most bolt-operated guns.

Shooting positions

The sniper must be fully conversant with as many firing positions as possible so that he has the maximum number of options when deployed on operations. Some positions may seem awkward and appear to break every rule on shooting, but the basic criterion is that if the sniper can consistently hit the target, then he should be left alone.

The prone position

This is the preferred shooting position of most shooters and is without doubt one of the steadiest. If at all possible, the sniper should adopt it or a modified version of it in all but hostile urban environments, where its lack of upward observation leaves him extremely vulnerable. This position will also allow the sniper to present the lowest profile of himself, except if using the Hawkins position (see below) and so improve his chances of remaining undetected.

Before firing, the sniper will go through the following check list in his head to ensure his position is correct and that he has considered all the elements that combine to make for a steady shooting position:

ABOVE: British and French Foreign Legion snipers train together in Kosovo in 2002. Knowing how to use other forces' equipment has served many soldiers over the years, and the ability to pick up another weapon and use it in war can be a life-saver.

BELOW: The author practicing with the Accuracy International suppressed sniper rifle during a sniper instructors' course at the British Army sniper school during his time as an instructor there. Suppressed sniper rifles are becoming increasingly prolific on operations today, so snipers must be fully versed in their uses.

The body. The body should be comfortable and lying slightly left of the line of fire [right for left handed firing].

Elbows. The elbows should always be a comfortable distance apart and this will vary from firer to firer. If the elbow is used to cradle the rifle butt then the shooter must ensure he is comfortable and that his breathing is not affected or restricted, as this can cause instability and a lowering of shooting standards.

Rifle support. The rifle must be supported by a combination of hands, the shoulder, and the chin. The weapon must be pulled back into the chin in order to support it, but over-stressing must be avoided as this will lead to an over-tension of the firer and a degradation of his ability to point the weapon naturally towards the target.

Firing hand. The firing hand is the primary supporting hand; its grip should be firm enough to support the rifle while avoiding over-grip, as this can lead to tension or strain, causing unsteadiness and fatigue.

Non-firing hand. This hand acts as a support for the weapon's butt or fore-stock. If a bipod is used this hand is usually placed up against the chest and clenched into a fist to support the butt. By keeping the fist in contact with the butt the sniper can raise or lower the position of the weapon by clenching or relaxing his fist.

Stock-weld. This is the instinctive ability of the sniper to place his cheek on the same point on the stock each time he adopts a fire position. This aids stability and comfort of the position and is something that is gained with practice and experience. It also ensures that the sniper has the correct eye relief relative to the telescopic sight.

Bone support. The sniper's body is the perfect framework to support his rifle, and is the foundation of the firing position.

Muscle relaxation. The purpose of using the bone framework to support the weapon is to allow the sniper to relax muscles, and thereby reduce unwanted movement caused by tense muscles. Any use of the muscles will generate movement in the sniper's position, hence the need for the position to be as comfortable as possible and thereby aid shooting performance.

Test and adjustment. The good shot will always test his position to ensure that the rifle points naturally towards the target. The way to ensure this is to adopt the fire position to be used and then close the eyes and take a few deep breaths. Upon opening the eyes the weapon's crosshairs should still be firmly across the intended target. If they are not, the body is not pointing naturally at the target and the position needs to be adjusted. The rifle is merely an extension of the sniper and by moving his body he will correct any faults in his position.

Practice. It is essential that the sniper spends a great deal of time practicing. This covers not only live-firing but also dry-training, where the sniper will go through the process of adopting a position and releasing the shot without actually firing a live round. This drill applies to all firing positions and should not be underestimated in its importance in sniper training.

The Hawkins position

This position is a modification of the basic prone firing position, in which the ground is used to support the rifle, thus enabling the sniper to present a lower profile. It is used when firing from low cover or folds in the ground and is a very steady firing platform, offering the sniper both stability and concealment. To adopt the Hawkins position the following modifications must be made to the basic prone position:

The body. The body is positioned much more to the left/right of the weapon than is usual. This can even become almost a right-angle to the line of the weapon.

Non-firing arm. This rests on the ground for the greater part of its length, with the hand holding the rifle by clenching a fist around the forward sling swivel. This means that the weapon is resting directly on top of the clenched fist.

The butt. The toe of the weapon butt should be resting on the ground, with the ground taking the full weight of the rifle and the butt tucked under the sniper's shoulder.

Recoil. By using the non-firing arm to maintain a forward pressure the rifle's recoil can effectively be controlled. The weapon should not be placed butt first against anything solid, as this may cause damage to the rifle.

BELOW: Sniping has changed very little over the years. As demonstrated by a sniper today, World War II equipment and weaponry are just as effective as they were then, while the laid-back shooting position is still taught to British snipers. There is a lack of alternate shooting position training in modern armies, and this is a mistake.

The laid-back position

The laid-back position has been in use for many years and was, indeed, a popular position with the early musketeers. It is of particular value when firing down slopes or when the sniper wishes to achieve a high degree of accuracy combined with an unconventional appearance.

The body. The sniper should lay on his side with his legs pointing towards the target and held together to provide support for the rifle. The legs also allow the sniper to raise or lower the point of aim by simply opening or closing the leg position. The weapon's butt should be in the shoulder and the non-firing hand should grasp the rifle in an overhand grip to provide stability.

Eye relief. With this position the eye relief is much greater than normal, and gives the sniper only a small floating aperture. It takes practice to center this reduced sight picture,

ABOVE: French Foreign Legion snipers train on the British Accuracy International sniper rifle during cross training on operational deployment. The rifles are covered in a light green fabric adhesive tape to allow any color to be applied without affecting the weapon, or upsetting the quartermaster!

but as long as the head is steady it is achievable. It is also advisable to rest or support the head on available cover or on a piece of equipment such as a rucksack.

Alternative firing positions

All recognized fire positions can be used when firing the sniper rifle. Some however will need modification to compensate for the change in center of balance associated with the extra length of the sniper rifle when compared to other smaller weapons.

Sitting position. This position can be adapted in several ways, each being a slight modification of the other:

Sitting open-legged. With this method the legs are kept a comfortable distance apart and the elbows are locked on the inside of the knees as low as possible. The body's weight should relax forward, and the marksmanship principles should be applied.

Sitting cross-legged. Exactly the same as the above, but with the exception of the legs being crossed at the ankles. The elbows can be rested either inside or outside the knees, whichever provides the firer with the most stable and comfortable position.

Sitting alternative. Both of the above

ABOVE: A French Foreign Legion sniper training in the seated firing position using an FRF 2 sniper rifle. He rests his elbows on the inner knee area to avoid the unstable bone-on-bone of elbow-to-knee and to allow support to be provided by the stronger muscles of the thighs.

BELOW: A French Foreign legion sniper being taught the British method of using an improvised tripod. He is also carrying out training under British supervision on the Accuracy International sniper rifle, known as the L96 in military service.

ABOVE: This French Foreign Legion sniper is practicing the laid-back position, which is ideal for forward slope positions. He is being trained in British shooting position techniques by snipers of 1 PWRR during an operational tour of the Balkans.

positions can be modified to suit the individual. The main variation is in the hold and support of the rifle. The variation can be as simple as bending the non-firing arm at the elbow so that the rifle rests along the top of the arm and the forearm rests on top of the knee. The other and more extreme variation is where the shin bone is used to support the weapon by the sniper wrapping his non-firing arm around the outside of the leg and pulling the weapon in against the leg for support. Due to the low level of the weapon in this position, the sniper is forced to invert his head and has an almost upside down sight picture and reduced aperture, similar to that of the laid-back position.

Sitting supported. The sniper uses this when some other form of support is available to carry the weight of the weapon, such as low cover, masonry or anything that will provide a platform for the weapon. Here the sniper can use this aid to provide extra stability for his shot, although with a fully floating barrel the sniper must be very careful not to rest the barrel in any way, as this will affect the fall of shot.

Kneeling position. This is best used only on level ground because any unevenness can lead to an unstable position and a loss of accuracy. It can be modified in many different ways but the basic position adopts the following parameters:

Right foot. The foot is placed in the most comfortable position possible with the sniper resting on his right knee and the foot rearwards. The right buttock is lowered onto the heel to avoid sitting too far back.

Left leg. The left leg is extended forward of the body with the toes pointing towards the intended target, foot flat on the ground. The non-firing elbow is rested on the left lower leg and the point of aim can be raised or lowered by movement of the left leg towards or away from the body.

Right elbow. The right elbow assumes a raised position to provide a natural cup to support the weapon butt.

Alternate kneeling. This position is very similar to the sitting alternate with the exception that the buttocks are raised off the ground. The head is still inverted and the left shin is still used as a support in conjunction with the non-firing arm that pulls it into the leg. This position requires practice and flexibility, and if mastered will provide a very stable shooting platform over all ranges.

Kneeling supported. This is as for the sitting supported, and any available cover or object is used to aid the overall stability of the firing position.

Standing position. The standing position is often ignored as it is difficult and should be avoided where possible, but this should not rule it out, as it may well turn out to be the only option available. While it can also be modified in various manners the basic stance is as follows:

Feet. The feet should always be placed at a comfortable distance apart, which is usually no more than shoulder width, with the feet angled approximately half right to the intended target.

Rifle butt. The butt is held slightly higher in the shoulder in this position in order to bring the sight into line with the naturally higher eye line.

Right elbow. The elbow should be pulled tight into the body to aid the support of the rifle, unless the sniper is engaging a moving target where it sometimes pays to keep the elbow higher and away from the body to avoid the tendency of pulling the barrel high right while tracking the target.

Right hand. This hand will provide the rifle with most of its support, which is achieved with a firm grip on the weapon stock or pistol grip.

Left hand. This can either adopt the traditional position on the fore stock or it can be clenched up and the arm bent at the elbow so as to rest the weapon along the top of the arm and hand, while resting the elbow on the hip or webbing in order to distribute the rifle weight and enable the position to be maintained longer.

Standing supported. This, as with all other supported positions, will rely upon other aids that may be available to help provide the firer with a more stable position.

Factors affecting application of fire

It is essential that snipers are aware of the factors that can affect their application of fire, and the easiest way to remember is by using the mnemonic FLAPWIW. This simple word will remind the sniper of the sub-headings of the factors he needs to check. The following are the main factors to remember:

F: Firing position. The mean point of impact (MPI) will vary slightly when firing from a different position from that in which the weapon was zeroed. This is caused by a combination of change in weapon harmonics, stability of position, and different pressures being placed upon the rifle. Good, well-built-up positions will reduce this effect.

L: Light. The light levels will affect how the sniper sees the target; he must remember how various light conditions will affect his view of the target and aim accordingly.

A: Attachments. Any attachment to the weapon will have an effect upon the weapon's harmonics. If the sniper intends to use attachments he should practice-fire the weapon and record the results, so as to provide him with settings for when he actually uses that attachment. Attachments can be night sights, lasers, and foliage, and all should be carefully checked before deploying on operations.

P: Positional support. The sniper must be aware that no matter what he uses to support the rifle, such as resting the weapon on his arm, the ground, or a tripod, it will have an

BELOW: German mountain snipers carry out long-range accuracy tests before moving up into the mountains and shooting across and down onto targets. They have ghillie camouflage suits for lower level sniping, and also improvised gray spray-painted mountain camouflage suits for the upper regions to assist in blending in with the rocks.

effect on his MPI and again he must train and record for this error. The sniper must never, under any circumstances, rest the barrel, as this will have a serious effect on his MPI.

W: Wind. The sniper must "read" the wind allow for the effects of wind on his shot.

I: Inefficient zero. For the sniper to cut corners or to mislead himself at the zeroing stage is to guarantee a problem further down the line, and if that happens to be on operations then it could cost him his life.

BELOW: The ghillie suit is at its best in close country, helping the sniper to deceive the enemy soldier's eye and memory combination: if the memory cannot recognize what the eye is showing it then the soldier will dismiss it and the sniper remains unseen.

W: Wet or oily ammunition. Wet or oily ammunition will cause an increase in chamber pressure. At worst this will cause an explosion or a bulge in the barrel, leading to a loss of accuracy in the weapon. At the very least it will result in increased muzzle velocity, thereby raising the MPI on the target.

Other factors affecting application of fire

Temperature. Under cold climate conditions the muzzle velocity will decrease, causing a lowering of the initial MPI, but each subsequent round will heat up the chamber, thus increasing the muzzle velocity and raising the MPI; the sniper must monitor for a climb and adjust accordingly. Higher than usual temperatures will have the opposite effect, causing the charge to burn much more rapidly, thus increasing the pressure and the muzzle velocity, and resulting in the round impacting higher on the target.

Humidity. The amount of moisture in the air will increase the drag on the bullet as it passes through it; the more moisture, the greater the resistance, causing the round to impact low on the target.

Rain. Heavy rain is always a problem for the sniper. The effect of wet ammunition and weapon parts has already been mentioned; every effort should be made to keep the weapon and ammunition dry. If this is not possible then it is better to allow the weapon to get totally wet and compensate by lowering the elevation setting. A cover or rain shield can be made and applied to the front and rear of the scope to reduce the levels of water getting to the lens, and a soft cloth should always be carried to assist in the removal of any rain that makes it to them.

Mirage. This is the effect of warm air rising off the earth's surface in the form of currents, and is most apparent on very warm days. The mirage will indicate any air movement on days when there is little or no wind and can be seen as ripples or waves rising from the ground. Judging for deflection takes much practice. The mirage is only a basic indication of air movement direction and not strength. When there is little or no wind it is known as "boiling mirage," and for any sideways movement it is called "drift." The sniper has to remember that his shot will almost definitely fly over the mirage effect, so the mirage is of only limited use to him and it should only be used to confirm some other more reliable method. But at longer ranges the mirage can at least give the sniper an indication of some form of wind movement at the target end.

Clothing. The sniper must be aware of how his clothing can affect his shooting ability and plan accordingly. The sniper must train from the very start of his shooting package in all of his operational ghillie kit, including suit, gloves, headgear, and webbing. Failing to do this will produce an inaccurate set of results in his logbook and hence will not be correct when applied on operations where the factors will have changed. This would seem to be an obvious point, but many training teams overlook it, leading to inconsistent shooting. The sniper must get used to his suit and modify it if necessary. He must also produce a logbook that gives the results and settings to be applied when in operational gear as opposed to results obtained while in comfortable uniform.

The poor shooting checklist

At some stage in his career the sniper will either have a bad day himself or will be training someone who could not hit an HMMWV at a hundred yards, all for no apparent reason. When this happens the first reference to call upon should be the poor shooting checklist and verify that:

- The sights are set correctly for elevation and deflection.
- The sight attachment screws are secure.
- The correct sight is fitted to the rifle.
- The sight drums are secure.
- The stock adjustments are secure.
- The bipod is not angled towards the target.
- The weapon is clean.

If all of the above fails to solve the problem, then the sniper should ask an experienced firer to shoot the weapon to check whether it is the weapon or the firer that is at fault, or get an armorer to carry out an inspection of the rifle.

Trigger control

The effort of getting into a good, stable fire position can be wasted in an instant if the sniper does not release the trigger at the correct time and in the correct manner. It is therefore essential that the trainee sniper be taught the fundamental skills of trigger control. The ability to release the shot without disturbing the aim is the basis of marksmanship and if the sniper cannot achieve this he will introduce inconsistency into his shooting and hence a loss of accuracy.

The action should be a smooth continuous movement and not a sharp jerk; jerking or snatching at the trigger is the most common fault in firers. Snatching is when the trigger is pulled too sharply and results in a disturbance of the position and the shot landing low right of the intended point of impact. As a guide, the best leverage for trigger operation is to pull from low down on the trigger and to use the middle of the finger as opposed to the tip, but as long as the sniper is comfortable and consistently hits the target any operation is acceptable.

Various aspects will affect the trigger operation; for the sniper to be effective it is essential that he is aware of these, as this will instill a sense of self-diagnosis for all his shots. The most common is that of flinching. This is when the sniper anticipates the shot and shies away from it, causing the position to break. The most effective way of overcoming this is for the instructor to load a mix of live and drill rounds on the range, without the sniper seeing the make-up of the

magazine. The sniper's reactions when firing should be monitored to see if he is flinching when he gets to a drill round and pulls away expecting to hear the weapon report. With this identified he can be coached through his problem using the same method. This type of drill must be monitored very carefully, with one instructor to each student to ensure range safety.

Another way to train for smooth trigger action is to place a coin on top of the barrel and get the sniper to operate the trigger. If the action is smooth the coin will stay in place; if

BELOW: A senior instructor from the German Mountain Warfare School checks the zero of his sniper rifle prior to moving up into the mountains during a training course. German mountain troops have a very well deserved reputation in this demanding area of combat.

not, it will fall away off. The sniper should be taught that there are two types of trigger control and that once he has overcome any hang-ups such as flinching, he will always use one or the other. These trigger actions are "interrupted" and "uninterrupted":

Interrupted. This is when the pressure on the trigger has been started and there is a pause, when the pressure is maintained, before continuing the pressure take-up until the moment of shot release. This is used with moving targets or when sight of the target is temporarily lost.

Uninterrupted. This, as the name suggests, is a continuous pressure on the trigger until the moment of shot release.

Breathing control

As with trigger operation, it is essential for the sniper to get his breathing correct prior to firing. The most natural time is that of the "natural respiratory pause." This is the point when the sniper has exhaled two-thirds of his lung capacity and has reached the natural pause in the breathing cycle—and is, thus, at the most relaxed point in the cycle. This period lasts for only a few seconds but can be extended to up to about eight seconds before the lack of oxygen begins to degrade the eyesight while also inducing discomfort and tension, affecting the stability of the sniper's position. This natural pause is the obvious point at which to release the shot and should also be used to perfect the aim, prior to taking two deep breaths to test and adjust the position before the moment of shot release. These techniques can only be mastered with constant practice with both live rounds and,

just as important, with dry training drills.

Grouping

It is essential that the potential snipers can effectively shoot a tight group when zeroing their personal weapons, since, if they cannot, the likelihood of them being able to engage targets at distance is highly questionable. The definition of a group can best be explained as the following:

- A series of shots, not less than three, fired from the same point and at the same point of aim will almost certainly never pass through the same hole and will more often produce a pattern of holes on the target forming a group.
- The reason that a poor grouper will be unlikely to hit targets at longer ranges is because:
- The size of the group will increase in direct proportion to the range.

With this in mind, if the firer can only achieve a four-inch group at a hundred yards then at six hundred yards he will probably group at twenty-four inches, and is therefore unlikely to hit a man-sized target. Thus, he is just not up to being trained as a sniper, no matter how keen he may be.

Shooting improvement options

In most armies the sniper is taught to shoot from many and varied positions in order to increase the chances of him being able to select a suitable fire position, no matter what the environmental surroundings, the results being accurately recorded in the sniper's logbook for future reference.

Apart from the prone or supported

positions, the sniper will find it increasingly difficult to maintain a stable shooting position for his weapon, so any assistance should be actively considered. Such assistance may include the abundance of weapon supports that are now available to the civilian hunter or shooter and could, under certain circumstances, be of use to the sniper. These weapon supports vary from collapsible bipods and tripods to very substantial and superbly stable shooting platforms. However, it is highly improbable that the military sniper, who has to enter the enemy's lair covertly, carrying his world about his person, will ever find a way to take such a luxury item with him, given its size and weight. For the police sniper the addition of one of these rests to the deployment vehicle is a must, as the stability provided for those long-drawn-out negotiation scenarios, where a sudden but highly accurate shot is required, cannot

be underestimated. Such weapon rests may also be a wise purchase for military anti-terrorist snipers, who may also find themselves in long-duration intelligence gathering operations and then be required to shoot with little warning.

The military sniper on the battlefield will rarely get the opportunity to use such precision-crafted shooting aids, as his world is a much harsher one and these items are just too big for sniper deployment. For him the word "improvise" comes once more to the fore, and again the sniper must create his own aids from what he can find.

U.S. and British forces have come up with two solutions. One is to take a normal camera tripod, with its light weight and height-adjusting legs, and simply add a weapon rest to

BELOW: During the early stages of a German Army mountain sniper course a student carries out zeroing practice on his personal weapon.

the camera platform, using sticky tape and sponge. This provides a good working platform from which to shoot, but is somewhat impractical inasmuch as it is awkward and cumbersome to carry or to stalk with under operational conditions. For urban operations, however, it may be worth the extra burden to provide the sniper with a ready-made rest that can be sited deep within a room.

The other and most used solution is that of cutting three suitably sturdy branches from around the area of operations and binding them together with parachute cord, approximately one-third down from the top of the branches. These can then be spread out to form a tripod on which to rest the rifle in order to provide a quick and sturdy rest from which to take the shot. The length of the branches will depend on the position the sniper intends to adopt, which in turn will be dictated by the available cover around his final fire position (FFP). A point of note when using this method is to ensure that the branches are cut away from the FFP and also, wherever possible, from a concealed position so as to not leave any indication or ground sign for the enemy to locate, as this may indicate the sniper's method of operation and endanger him or his colleagues at a later date.

BELOW: A sniper pauses to take stock of his location and tactical position during a training exercise, using the low bush behind him to aid his concealment.

Snap shooting

The military sniper will usually be patrolling in close proximity to the enemy and may, therefore, on occasion need to engage them at short notice, while a police sniper may arrive on a scene and not have time to make a prepared shot. In both situations the sniper must make the most of the flatter trajectory of the closer ranges and set his sights on three hundred yards for the military and a hundred yards for the police sniper. The reason for this is that at this setting the sniper can aim at the center of a man-sized target at any range between a hundred and four hundred yards and, due to the flatter trajectory, expect to hit the target.

Miss drills

If a sniper finds that he is missing the target he must locate the fall of shot in order to adjust his fire back on to the target. To do this the sniper and his observer can use one of the following methods:

Strike/splash. This is the ground kicked up by the bullet's impact and indicates the fall of shot.

Swirl. This is the air that is displaced by the bullet as it travels towards the target, and is seen as a swirling vortex that indicates the bullet's path.

Glint. Under certain conditions it is possible to see a glint of light reflected off the bullet as it travels through the air, and this, although brief, will indicate the likely fall of shot.

Tracer. While not a recommended method

as the tracer round damages the weapon bore and may lead to loss of accuracy, tracer rounds can be used as a last resort.

Wind allowance

The sniper must both understand the prevailing wind's effects and also be able to make allowances for its influence in order to hit his intended target, especially over the greater distances that he will shoot. Learning all about the wind's effects and how to allow for them will take the sniper many hours of practice; keeping an accurate logbook with details of different types of wind effect will assist in building up a solid database for future shoots.

The wind can influence the sniper twice when shooting: once by affecting the firer's ability to hold the weapon stable prior to shot release, and, second, by affecting the bullet as it passes through the air. The sniper can offset the first by adopting a suitably stable fire position, but the ability to judge for the effect on the bullet takes more time to master.

The wind effect at the target end is often misleading, since by the time the bullet has reached that point, it has already been affected, so the sniper needs to judge the wind within the first half of his bullet's flight. There are four main factors that he will have to allow for:
• Wind strength (velocity).
• Wind direction.
• Range to the target.
• The bullet (size, weight and velocity).

Wind strength. The wind's strength has to be determined in order for the sniper to calculate its effect on his shot. There are generally five recognized wind strengths that are used in these equations. They are:

- Gentle—5mph. Wind barely felt, but just detectable.
- Moderate—10mph. Wind felt lightly on the face; leaves and twigs moving.
- Fresh—15mph. Wind moves dust, paper; small branches on trees in constant motion.
- Strong—20mph. Wind moves the majority of the tree.
- Very strong—25mph+. Wind moves large trees; telephone wires hum in the wind.

Apart from these visible signs on natural objects, the sniper is sometimes advised to drop some grass from the firing point and observe the angle at which it falls to the ground; obviously, the further from him it lands the stronger the wind, while the spot where it lands indicates the direction. This, however, only indicates the wind at the firing point and not further out along the bullet's flight-path and so is of limited value; and, in any case, there seems little point in dropping grass while the sniper is in the prone position.

Another, often quoted, method of gauging the wind is to note the angle of the range flag. This might be of some use on the rifle range, but an enemy on the battlefield or a terrorist holed up in a city is very unlikely to display a flag for the benefit of the sniper who is trying to kill him!

Wind values

The wind direction will also have an effect on the bullet in flight, and so is just as important as the strength. To determine wind value the easiest method to use is the clock method. This places an imaginary clock over the sniper's view and is broken down into sections, with each section having a different wind value depending on its effect on the bullet's flightpath. The direction that will have the most significant effect on the bullet is that of a wind blowing left to right or right to left (i.e., at 90 degrees) across the bullet's path, and so will be recorded as the highest or "full value." This will be three to nine or nine to three on the clock face. For wind blowing at oblique angles, such as from one to seven or from eleven to five, a value of half the right-to-left wind is given ("half value"). For a wind blowing directly into the sniper's face or over him and directly towards the target a "zero value" is given, as these will have little if any effect on the bullet's path.

Most armies issue their snipers with a wind calculation table, and these are generally committed to memory. They follow a basic formula with the range, wind direction, and strength all laid out in a simple graph format that enables the sniper to quickly equate the solution he needs; for oblique winds he simply halves the total he reached on his calculation for a "full value" wind.

As elsewhere, the ability to judge the wind strength accurately and decide on the effect on the shot only comes with constant practice, although, as with judging distance,

RIGHT: The ability to identify and use dead ground (i.e., ground the enemy cannot see) is a vital one for the sniper. Here a sniper pair use a crease in the ground to move below the line of sight of the enemy, and hence remain undetected.

there are just a few very fortunate people who have a natural skill in this area.

Moving targets

The ideal target, when shooting over any sort of distance, is static and on a windless day—but life is seldom perfect. A type of engagement more frequently encountered is a moving target that the sniper loses lost sight of every couple of seconds. Thus the sniper must be competent with moving as well as static targets in order to be effective. As with normal shooting practices, there are two ways of engaging moving targets:

• Tracking method. This involves the sniper aligning with the required lead for the target, maintaining it, and releasing the shot when ready, ensuring that he follows through, otherwise the shot will strike to the rear of the target and miss.

• Ambush method. With this method, the sniper selects a point ahead of the target's direction of travel and releases the shot when the lead is reached for that particular target.

Engaging moving targets is a difficult skill to acquire and, as with so many other areas of sniping, it requires constant and dedicated practice. However, there are some common mistakes that, once identified, can be overcome:

• A tendency to jerk or snatch the trigger at the moment of shot release, caused by the sniper anticipating the shot and trying to "force" it; this is most commonly associated with the ambush method.

• Failure to add adjustments for deflection to allow for wind influence; many snipers

overlook this requirement when preoccupied with the moving target.

- The sniper may focus on the target and not the sight reticule, and hence not pay attention to his lead point within the sight's reticule pattern.

All of these points can be easily remedied and just require the sniper to think a bit harder and to not be seduced by the moving target and then forget the basics of engaging distance targets.

Target leads

As with many areas of the sniper's skills, the leads taken for moving targets will vary from firer to firer as people have different levels of reaction, and trigger-pull upon locating their target. But there is a general starting system that is applied by many of the world's snipers. This system is very similar to that used in the calculation of the wind's effects and follows the principle of identifying start values for walking targets, with these values being doubled for a running target and halved for an oblique target.

This method allows for a five "minute of angle" (MOA) lead for a walking man at ranges between four hundred and six hundred yards, and can be applied by aiming ahead of the target (the "lead") or by applying the calculation to the sight and maintaining point of aim/point of impact. The settings for a moving target must be applied only after allowance has been made for the effects of the wind, and it may well be that to allow for a moving target some of the setting just applied for wind has then to be removed again. For example, a man moving at walking speed (3mph or 5 MOA) traveling right to left across the sniper's view would cancel out an adjustment of 5 MOA added for a left to right wind. This method allows the sniper to aim at the center of the target and maintain point of aim/point of impact.

In the aiming off method, these adjustments are again calculated for a walking target and need to be doubled for fast targets and halved for oblique targets, accordingly. Using the 5 MOA method, the sniper will take the first figure of the range to the target and multiply it by five to give the lead required; for example, 5 x 600 yards = 30-inch lead. As with the previous method, adjustments for wind should be applied first and then for movers, with the aim point at the required position ahead of the target.

Suppressed capability

The additional ability to fire reduced-noise-level rounds is one that all snipers should have. Most current sniper rifles are available in suppressed versions. This area of shooting is again one that is instinctively linked to the world of Special Forces and assassins, but if looked at it in a realistic and tactical way, it becomes obvious why the sniper should have suppressed capability on all deployments. The sniper often passes within feet of the enemy or has to move past an enemy to reach his target, so the ability to limit the number of people who hear his shot will limit the number of people who come looking for him, and hence greatly increase his safety. The suppressed sniper rifle is a strange weapon and requires a lot of practice to master, but once this is done it is just as devastating in effect as its full bore brother, maybe even more so, since for an enemy to see someone drop beside him and yet hear nothing can have a very far-reaching psychological impact.

Destruction drills

All snipers must be taught how to destroy their weapons in the event of capture or having to abandon their rifles in order to prevent the enemy from using the weapons for their own nefarious purposes. The following are effective methods of rendering a rifle useless:

- Block the barrel with earth, sand, metal or anything that will do the job; push the muzzle firmly and as deep as possible into the ground and then, using string, pull the trigger to fire the weapon.
- Strip the weapon and hide or bury parts over a wide area.
- Strip the weapon and keep essential parts after abandoning the rifle.
- Take any steps necessary to bend the barrel, smash the telescopic sights, and generally destroy the weapon's accuracy.

BELOW: A French Foreign Legion warrant officer briefs his snipers on their task during a cross training period with the British snipers of 1PWRR. It is essential to take the time at the beginning of any operation to plan and confirm all details of the operation.

SNIPER SHOT PLACEMENT

One aspect of sniping that is of increasing importance is anti-materiel shot placement: the targeting of equipment, machines, and vehicles that can include anything from airfield radars, generators, main battle tanks, crew-served weapons, to military and civilian aircraft, and even warship weapons and communications systems. There is an abundance of information on where to place a shot for the maximum effect on the human target—with graphic diagrams of the human brain and other parts of the anatomy—and what the impact from high velocity ammunition will do to it. However, there is very little literature focusing on what happens to machines and weaponry when impacted by high-speed lead. There is certainly a need to provide our own military snipers and law enforcement officers with information and instruction on anti-materiel targeting, while it is also as important to raise the awareness of defense forces to the current vulnerability of vital equipment—both military and civilian—to attack from the sniper's bullet.

Land force targets

Traditionally, armored vehicles and tanks have been seen as the ultimate warfighting machines, impervious to attack from small arms fire. Indeed, many books on these

BELOW: When supported by a battle group main battle tanks still rule the battlefield, but alone and without support they become vulnerable. Snipers with the right training and therefore knowledge can be a serious threat to the tank.

weapons describe them as having total protection from small arms and mine damage. This may be true from the viewpoint of the crew under armor, but it is not true for the tank itself.

The tank, or indeed any armored vehicle, is a claustrophobic place in which to work; therefore crews spend most of their time with their head and upper body stuck up out of the armor protection. This lends itself nicely to sniper attack and, as the tank is only as effective as its crew, remove the crew and the tank is useless. The noise level associated with working in armor means that crew members must wear ear defense and intercom systems in order to communicate, and this in itself restricts their hearing. Hot, and with restricted hearing, the crew members exposed in the turrets present the sniper with the opportunity to eliminate them with rapid-bolt manipulation or successive shots with a semiautomatic sniper rifle before the second target has realized why his partner has slumped forward. At worst, if the second crewman has become aware of the fact that they are under fire, the turret is left manned by one crew member who is now battened down and has restricted viewing options.

Tanks today have an array of optical and thermal camera systems that can make the novice sniper a very easy target, but for the experienced or well-trained sniper these systems are of limited threat. The majority of these systems rely upon optical lenses that have to be directed towards a target in order for it to be located, and in doing so they present the sniper with a clear line of fire against the optic and therefore a chance to destroy the optic itself and the effectiveness of the system. Some armies have already recognized this problem, mainly due to war debris and hits from disgruntled stone throwers in security operations, and have fitted limited mesh screens to protect the lenses. But this will be of little use against a sniper who exercises pinpoint accuracy or, worse still, uses a 338- or .50-caliber weapon.

In addition to the optical units, the

BELOW: Armor and the highly trained crews at work are a dream come true for a roaming sniper team, since a tank is only as effective as the crew inside it. Without a crew, a tank is nothing more than a large metal box!

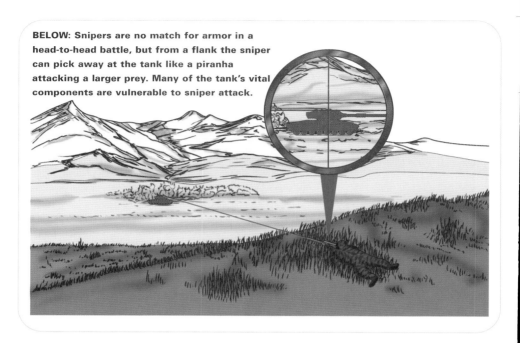

BELOW: Snipers are no match for armor in a head-to-head battle, but from a flank the sniper can pick away at the tank like a piranha attacking a larger prey. Many of the tank's vital components are vulnerable to sniper attack.

BELOW: Armored vehicle crews have a very stupid habit of sitting outside the protection of their vehicle, and many have recently paid the price by being hit by sniper fire. The armor can only protect the crew if they are inside, and by forcing them inside the sniper affects their observation and morale in one step.

modern tank is fitted with an array of antenna and sensors required for the tank's fire control system. These enable it to engage targets while on the move and at extreme ranges. If they are damaged or destroyed, the crew must return to the old calculated method of firing, and the time and accuracy penalties that go with it, reducing the tank's effectiveness. With the use of .50-caliber sniper rifles, areas such as running gear, engine, and fuel cells become a credible target for the sniper, and another opportunity to reduce a tank's ability to fight.

With the correct training in recognition and shooting, the sniper has the ability to engage armor from maximum range, reduce its effectiveness, and increase its vulnerability to other weaponry. The sniper is one part of a layered defense and not an answer to all problems, and so should be sited in conjunction with supporting weaponry to achieve maximum effect.

ABOVE: The modern battle tank is a fearsome beast and one that takes no prisoners in a one-to-one battle. The sniper, however, has the accuracy to render important parts of the tank inoperable with well placed armor-piecing shots. The more external optics and antenna placed on the tank, the greater number of targets for the sniper.

ABOVE: Targets on a tank, such as sights and sensors, are easy to identify, and many have protected covers and armor plate, but to use them the systems the protective doors have to be open, and they are then vulnerable to damage from sniper fire.

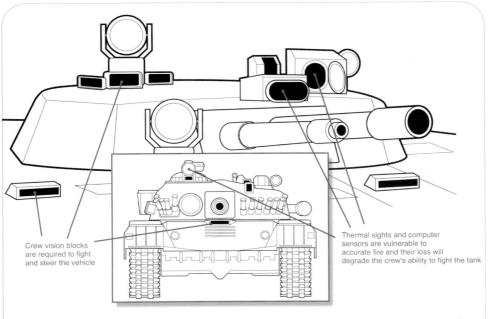

Crew vision blocks are required to fight and steer the vehicle

Thermal sights and computer sensors are vulnerable to accurate fire and their loss will degrade the crew's ability to fight the tank

ABOVE: Such areas as commander and driver vision blocks, commander's sight, gunner's sight, thermal and other optical devices, computer mast, and external protection devices are all legitimate targets for the sniper.

Armored personnel carriers

Targeting armored personnel carriers (APCs) is another area where the correct siting and interlocking of supporting weaponry arcs will maximize the potential of the sniper attack. APCs have much lighter protective armor than main battle tanks (MBTs) and as such are easier to penetrate using small arms and missile systems. The crews suffer from the same tendency to expose themselves above the armor protection and therefore to sniper fire. While thermal and optical systems are becoming available on newer APCs, it is still mainly MBTs that have these; once forced to batten down, the crew have limited ability to view the battlefield. This in itself reduces the effectiveness of the vehicle and increases the attack potential of a ground-based enemy force, showing again

ABOVE: Protective doors can only protect when closed, and if closed they are not in use. External additions to modern armored vehicles are usually of importance to the fighting ability of the vehicle, and therefore to damage or destroy them will affect the capabilities of the vehicle.

how snipers can affect the balance of probability on the battlefield.

With the advent of the .50-caliber weapon and armor-piercing high-explosive or incendiary ammunition, lighter armored vehicles are now vulnerable to destruction, as discovered in both the first and second Gulf Wars, when Allied snipers utilized these weapons.

Soft-skin vehicles (un-armored)

The ability to engage and kill the crews of supply vehicles such as troop-carrying, re-

supply or fuel trucks has always been known, but not so the active deployment of snipers in such attacks behind an enemy lines. Identifying and attacking enemy supply is a recognized Special Forces task, but one that sniper teams could just as easily carry out, releasing the SF for more arduous and tactical roles. Un-armored vehicles are vulnerable to all forms of ammunition available to the sniper, and either the crew or the vehicles themselves can be targeted for destruction, depending on the rules of engagement and the tactical value to be gained from each.

ABOVE: A Greek armored personnel carrier in Kosovo in 2002. Static, and with limited rapid movement options, and with the crew exposed, it would make a perfect target for armor-piecing flash incendiary ammunition from a .50-caliber rifle.

BELOW: The sniper knows that any troops inside a vehicle are going to exit at some point, especially if under attack, so positioning himself to engage the troop doors is always a good option. Many rear doors are of thinner armor or contain fuel, and so increase in target value.

Missile systems

As with naval missile systems, land-based systems are just as vulnerable to damage from high-speed metal impact, and so are a target for sniper weapons of all calibers. Each missile system is made up of several required parts, such as missile launcher, tracker radar,

and target location equipment, and all of these parts are essential to the overall operational effectiveness of the missile system. If trained to recognize these elements and different systems the sniper is able to locate and identify essential missile components and apply effective rifle fire to reduce or destroy their ability to operate. The location radar has mechanical gearing, a receiver, and dish as well as banks of circuit boards, all of which are easily damaged by accurate fire. The missile launcher has both mechanical systems and the explosive missiles themselves to target, and the control unit has circuitry

ABOVE: On many of today's tanks the driver is protected by raised armor to the flanks, but only one or two vision blocks, so if forced to batten down by enemy fire he has limited vision abilities to drive the tank. Damaging or destroying those ports by sniper fire would seriously impair the vehicle.

BELOW: Lack of attention to detail gives away the armored vehicle as the flat-plate armored glass is reflecting in the tree line a few feet below the truck, making it as visible as the truck that is sky-lined. Had the glass been covered an enemy may have regretted attacking the obvious target in this scenario.

BELOW LEFT: Many of today's AFVs have armor-plated glass driver and commander windows with drop-down metal armor cover. A sniper using a .50-caliber rifle will not allow the crew the luxury of time to drop these covers, and so the vehicle is vulnerable.

and power supplies to attack, not to mention the crew. Using snipers armed with .50-caliber weapons to attack tactical systems such as Scud missiles and their launchers, and newer systems, is not only cheaper than an aircraft-delivered smart weapon, but it is easier to deploy and recover and presents the enemy with limited options for retaliation.

Anti-aircraft artillery, heavy artillery, and mortars

In Somalia, East Africa, in the mid-1990s, the U.S. Marine Corps deployed and used their sniper assets to locate, identify, and eliminate the AAA threat to friendly helicopter forces. The marines regard their sniper teams as an integral part of the offensive options available to the commander. This trust comes from an understanding at commander level due to the education of

ABOVE: The Scud mobile ballistic missile launcher has been the archetypical target: the missile is only effective if it leaves the launcher and for that to happen the crew must program it, and this leaves the missile vulnerable. Removing the crew or damaging the computer suite area will leave the missile exactly what it is in this picture, a museum piece.

ABOVE: The glass areas in the center and to the right of this mobile anti-aircraft missile system are both at risk from sniper attack. The optics locate the target and guide the missile, while the crewman's location is very exposed. For a close-up look at much of your intended target, just visit a local military show and crawl all over it!

LEFT: Modern radar systems can be damaged by high-impact ammunition; they are usually located away from frontline troops, and so are vulnerable to sustained sniper attack. By removing a radar, a sniper team may in fact remove a much larger asset, such as missile or gun systems.

marine officers early in their careers with regard to sniper options.

Artillery units have long been aware of the threat posed to them from counter fire and aircraft, but the prospect of an enemy sniper hunter team actively seeking out their positions is one that is often overlooked, but one that has existed since the days of the Dutch Boers sniping so effectively against the highly visible British forces in the late 19th century. As with many other weapons today, the artillery piece is vulnerable to accurate fire against its crew as well as the locating radar and mobile computer systems used to speed up accurate artillery fire. If the

BELOW: Crew-served weapons have always been a favorite of the sniper; without them many units would be seriously depleted of heavy firepower. If the crews are under cover due to sniper fire, it means the weapon is not in use, and so the sniper has scored a success!

crews are pinned down or forced to revert to infantry counter-attack drills to remove a sniper threat, then the supporting fire they would otherwise provide cannot take place.

USMC .50-caliber sniper attack

Early in the 1991 Gulf War, in order to remove an Iraqi artillery threat to their own forces, the U.S. Marines deployed two sniper pairs armed with Barrett .50-caliber sniper rifles. The snipers approached under cover of darkness to within 1,750 yards of the enemy. They used accurate fire to destroy both the hand controls and the recuperators on the artillery pieces, rendering them useless. Using armor-piercing incendiary ammunition they also engaged the munitions stockpile and rapidly set it ablaze, causing Iraqi casualties.

The Iraqis used the 100mm main armament of a tank located near the artillery to engage the snipers' likely positions, and employed a soldier on top of the tank to look for the flash of the snipers' weapons. The snipers shot him with one round and returned to base unscathed, leaving behind several damaged artillery pieces, destroyed ammunition stockpiles, and many dead and injured, all for the cost of several .50-caliber rounds.

Radar and security systems

Most military forces today have some form of ground radar or other security surveillance system in place to warn of enemy movement or approach. These systems are again made up of component parts, each interlocked and essential to the other for the system to function properly. With a good standard of recognition training, the sniper is able to locate and identify the individual parts of such systems and target them from long ranges. As with all of today's technological battlefield assets, the systems are equipped for general knocks and drops but are not armored against small arms fire. Therefore accurate rifle fire is all but certain to destroy or seriously damage the equipment, or at least degrade its operational abilities. Most systems are made up of individual, linked sensors predictably placed out to provide area coverage. If damaged or

ABOVE: Special Forces are always at risk from snipers. The fact that they wear different uniforms and carry different weaponry readily identifies them; while they would not be stupid enough to operate as openly as here, snipers have night optics too!

BELOW: Associated equipment for larger crew-served weapons systems is also a good target for the sniper, who is not likely to stop the weapon being employed, but will make it harder and more time consuming for the crew to deploy and fire the weapons.

they go off line, they will be visited by a maintenance team, who also become sniper targets. The other decidedly weak link in the system is the very vulnerable and highly trained crew, who are difficult to replace at short notice. With a period of observation by a sniper team, it would be possible to identify all members of the control team and eliminate them all during a period of sustained attack prior to targeting the equipment.

Radio and other communication systems

A military force is only as effective as its command and control system. The opening moves of the second Gulf War were to disrupt the Iraqi command's ability to communicate with its forces, and hence remove the ability to organize an effective defense.

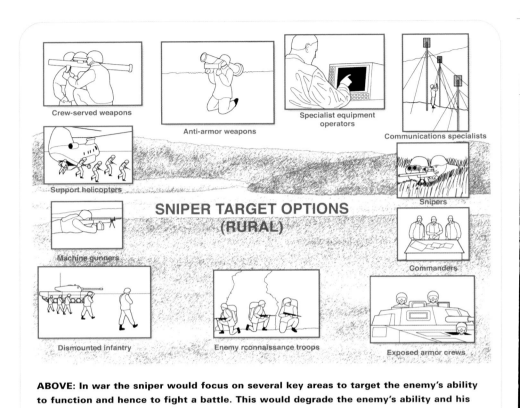

Crew-served weapons

Anti-armor weapons

Specialist equipment operators

Communications specialists

Support helicopters

SNIPER TARGET OPTIONS (RURAL)

Snipers

Machine gunners

Commanders

Dismounted infantry

Enemy rconnaissance troops

Exposed armor crews

ABOVE: In war the sniper would focus on several key areas to target the enemy's ability to function and hence to fight a battle. This would degrade the enemy's ability and his will to fight.

This procedure can apply for any level of military force, from brigade down to an infantry section. This fact makes being a military communications specialist a very hazardous position, as he becomes a much sought-after asset for a sniper team on the hunt. Most of the battlefield radios used today are no stronger than their World War II predecessors, and as such do not have robust resistance to fragmentation or direct fire. The equipment of communications specialists has antenna, pole, trailing-wire or HF wire systems, and these are all easy to locate by the observation-trained sniper teams. Once located, it is only a matter of time before the sniper identifies the operator and attacks either the equipment or the operator, or both.

Crew-served weapons

Snipers are a very real threat to any crew-served weapon, such as anti-tank missiles and heavy machine guns, and their teams. These weapons can inflict severe damage on the snipers' friendly forces and as such are high on the snipers' list of targets to be located and destroyed. Most crew-served weapons have long range, so the weapon teams foolishly feel they are out of sniper range and safe from attack. They therefore never cam-

RIGHT: Communications is the key to winning a battle, as he who communicates best and quickest is likely to be at an advantage. To target the technicians and equipment that make this possible is a major function of the sniper: if the enemy can't talk to his troops, he can't maneuver them either. Just ask Saddam!

ouflage their positions. This makes them very easy to locate for a trained sniper observer with a powerful optic. The weapons are slow-moving and cumbersome, and the crews become fatigued and lazy, adopting sloppy drills. Vehicle-mounted systems are mostly of the bolt-on variety and cannot be fired or re-loaded under armor, leaving the crews exposed to sniper attack in the same way that dismounted crews are.

BELOW: Heavy machine guns are as devastating today as they have ever been and as such both the men and machines are key targets for removal by the sniper.

Support equipment

The target list for the anti-materiel sniper is almost endless, and the ability of an enemy, on the battlefield or in a city, to function when it keeps losing all its ancillary support machinery to accurate small arms fire is vastly reduced. For example, communications units are powered either by batteries or generator-

ABOVE: Even attacking the equipment element of a specialized vehicle such as the crane mechanism can be enough to slow or stop repair work on an armored column. With a sniper pair on the prowl it is unlikely that much work would get done around here anyway!

ABOVE: Armored recovery vehicles and their crews are a very high prize target for the sniper teams, as without these technicians the highly temperamental vehicles are left high and dry in a very mobile battle zone.

ABOVE: The laid-back attitude and working environment of technical support units are ideal for the snipers. Once attacked, the morale and fear factor among these rear echelon troops will seriously hinder any maintenance and hence the ability of the frontline troops to deploy.

produced electricity, and the generators produce the power to run the battery chargers. If snipers identify and destroy these pieces of vital machinery with rifle fire this will cause all manner of problems for the unit and degrade its ability to carry out its job. This in turn will affect other units in different ways. Here lies the sniper's ability to affect a much wider area than would normally appear possible. Generators would be a major target for the anti-materiel sniper team in many different locations, from naval ports to airfields, where vital day-to-day activity centers around larger machinery being powered or started by mobile generators. The sniper team commander who does not spend time on a wide and diverse level of recognition training will limit the potential of his teams.

Commanders/leaders

The skill of shot placement, and knowing where to shoot to do the most damage to the enemy, are as applicable to anti-personnel shooting as to targeting weapons and equipment. Snipers should be trained to develop the skill of being able to watch the enemy and in a short time to identify and kill the man or men the others look up to. The target chosen may not be the highest rank, or the brains of the gang, but he will be the one they all believe is invincible or the best soldier around; so to kill him will destroy morale and induce widespread fear. Being able to identify the target—he could be the one being given the first food or drink, or the

ABOVE: A sniper's view of a rear echelon base area whose personnel are totally unaware that they are being observed and targeted by unseen eyes. This scene is a unit deployed to Kosovo that provided British snipers with a training opportunity—although the "targets" wouldn't have known it until now, if they are reading this!

man delegating tasks to others—is an important skill for sniper teams.

Human shot placement

The area of shot placement on a human target will be wholly dependent upon the results the sniper wishes to achieve. For the military sniper, most targets will best serve the sniper's needs by suffering a life-threatening injury that requires medical attention and evacuation, all of which necessitate the involvement of additional manpower and apply restrictions on the enemy support system. This would indicate a center of mass shot against human targets, which, at long range, will normally result in at least a chance of survival, reducing as the range from firer to victim decreases due to the available kinetic energy left in the round when it impacts.

BELOW: This human target is actually a helicopter pilot who has no idea he is facilitating the training of snipers; an aircraft is only as effective as the pilot in it, and if he is without his head the aircraft is of no use!

In a law enforcement or counter-sniper scenario there is a requirement to make sure that the target dies instantaneously. There is therefore only one area to target, the head, and to be specific the brain stem, or the join between the spinal column and the brain. This is the only place that the target can be hit where all possibility of muscular or reflex action is negated. When viewing the target from the front, a shot impact between the nose and the top lip will do the required damage, as the shock wave that follows the bullet will destroy the brain stem, even if the bullet is deflected. From the side, the bullet needs to impact around the lower ear to achieve the same results, and from the rear the bullet should impact at the base of the

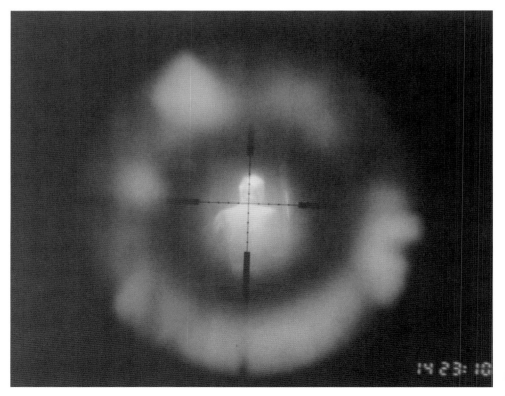

ABOVE: Air shows are a fantastic source of sniper-related knowledge and reconnaissance, and every sniper should attend as many shows as he can to obtain pictures and information on potential targets.

skull in between the two tendons that support the head and neck.

Airfield targets

The wide expanse of the average airfield, be it military or civilian, lends itself to the skills and range of the stand-off sniper. The general perception of a sniper attack is one where an individual is killed with a single round fired from long range. This is far from the limit of the sniper. Aircraft, and the associated support machinery, are all very technical and by definition expensive. They are also very easy to damage or destroy with the high-speed impact of metal. Generators are obvious targets, but the airfield is a veritable feast for the anti-materiel sniper team.

Aircraft

An aircraft is a complex machine that is particularly vulnerable to direct action attack. Gone are the days when aircraft could take a lot of hits and still fly, and the reason for this lies in both the materials and the technology used to keep them in the air. Many of today's high-tech aircraft could not be flown without the computer systems that are fitted. If the sniper understands the aircraft's internal make-up and the equipment it cannot function without, he will know where best to place his shots to destroy the aircraft or temporarily remove it from service. There is much information in the public domain on aircraft, their systems, and support equipment. Public air shows also allow the snipers to get up close to possible target

71

aircraft. Here they can even ask aircrew veiled questions in order to further their knowledge. Sniper commanders therefore should get their platoons out on field trips to air displays and get learning!

Targets will depend upon the type of aircraft to be attacked. Fighters and attack aircraft are by nature smaller, and have a lot of vital equipment crammed in to them. Transports and patrol aircraft are larger, and so a more detailed knowledge of their inner layout will be needed to target specific equipment. All aircraft, however, have common vital areas that can be attacked, and you don't need to be a rocket scientist to identify parts that the aircraft just cannot do without.

BELOW: Air shows feature a wide range of aircraft on static display; you may not be allowed to get into or on the aircraft but you will be able to get within camera range, and with modern digital cameras the results will be good enough to produce useful Powerpoint lessons and planning packs.

LEFT: For a sniper to get this close to high tech aircraft, such as this F/A-18 Hornet, is almost a dream come true; he can study the strengths and weaknesses, such as the nose cone where the main radar is located, the wings, and the engine area.

RIGHT: The AH-64 Apache is a weapon system feared all over the world, except in Iraq where the enemy just uses multiple RPG rounds to bring it down! So the message is that, hard-hitting though the Apache may be, it is vulnerable to a sniper who will find the sensor pack on the nose and the rotor area easy targets that will cripple the aircraft.

BELOW: Hits in the cockpit area of a modern aircraft are almost certain to strike vital systems and reduce the aircraft's operational capabilities. Even the front wheel system is vulnerable and without it the aircraft is going nowhere.

Nose wheel. All aircraft require strong and functional front wheel mechanisms in order to taxi around, let alone rapidly accelerate down a runway to achieve takeoff speed. Any hit in this area from either .338- or .50-

caliber weaponry would be capable of causing enough damage to stop the aircraft from being operational until inspections and repairs are carried out. Even shooting out of tires will lead to a major hold-up in aircraft operations while changes are carried out.

Nose cone. The nose cone of any aircraft usually holds some form of radar dish and equipment vital to the aircraft's operational role. Firing metal into and through it will inevitably caused damage to the system. The nose cone is also a vital part of any aircraft's aerodynamic

shape, so to disfigure and break it will have a major effect on how, if at all, the aircraft will fly.

Cockpit/lower front section. The cockpit of any modern aircraft is packed with computers and circuit boards, not to mention hydraulic and electrical systems,

BELOW: The hovering support helicopter is an easy target for the sniper team and if it is full of enemy troops all the better. Hits in the rotor or main body area will have an effect on the aircraft and crew. The cockpit area also offers at least two soft pilots to target.

and the lower forward section of the aircraft is similarly equipped. Hits in these areas are almost guaranteed to damage vital equipment, sufficient to remove the aircraft from operations. Impact damage to the actual cockpit canopy will also cause a delay in operations since the plane would not be able to take off and operate effectively.

Central section and engines. The central section of the aircraft carries the engines in smaller tactical aircraft, and work or storage areas in larger types that have wing-mounted engines. Engines are a mass of precision-made metal parts, from fan blades to transfer pipes, and all are easily damaged by accurate rifle fire. High-speed impacts from birds can cause serious enough damage to shut down an engine, or even bring down the aircraft completely, and this should give an indication as to the potential damage a rifle-fired projectile could cause. From the frontal aspect the sniper is presented with the fan blades that are essential for drawing air into and through the jet. Damage can be caused to an engine by high-speed ingestion of fractured fan blades or debris while the engine is in motion; and if the sniper targets the blades while the engine is switched off it could not be started safely. Again, trade shows and open days at military bases will allow the sniper to take a close-up look at engines with and without their protective cowlings in place.

An area also of interest in the smaller tactical aircraft, but often overlooked, is directly behind the cockpit canopy. Here are often stored electronic systems vital to the aircraft's fighting capabilities, so this area is worth a round or two by the sniper. On many aircraft this area also houses the canopy mechanism, and if you cannot open or close the cockpit, you can't fly the aircraft!

Wings. Ailerons and flaps on aircraft wings, together with electronic controls, can be damaged by small arms fire, gravely affecting the aircraft's ability to function. Sections of the wings often serve as fuel tanks, so incendiary ammunition fired into these has a good chance of causing destruction through fire and explosion.

Main undercarriage. The undercarriage is a complex combination of moving parts and provides the sniper with a clear way to restrict the aircraft's operational use. Even if this causes just a few hours loss of operational service, that may be enough if the sniper's objective is to clear the way for other forces to attack. Unlike the family car, jacking up an aircraft is not as straightforward as it may seem, and if the sniper then targets the repair crew and tools he can prolong the agony.

Tail section. Many aircraft have electronic equipment positioned in the tail section, including defensive suites and electronic surveillance systems. Damaging these will impair or eliminate the aircraft's ability to deploy. The rear control surfaces are also as important as those on the main wings, and could become useful additional targets for snipers.

Defensive aid suites. Defensive systems are fitted to help protect aircraft from heat-seeking and radar-guided missiles. These systems vary from electronic emitting units to high-intensity flare dischargers. The sniper should learn to identify these units and target them accordingly. The flares are designed to convince an incoming missile that they are in fact the aircraft engines; if they can be initiated while still attached to the aircraft this will undoubtedly cause damage and may lead to secondary fire problems for the defender.

Airfield support equipment

In addition to targeting aircraft, a well-trained sniper team can cause havoc to the infrastructure and operational capabilities of an airfield. No work area, military or civilian, can function if persistent interference restricts the day-to-day functions of its staff. This disruption can be caused by direct targeting of the staff, or by the destruction of or damage to associated tools and machinery needed by those staff.

Hangars and repair facilities. The large and often open-ended facilities needed to run the constant maintenance of aircraft are obvious targets for the sniper team. Not only are these

ABOVE: The airfield infrastructure is as much of a target as the aircraft themselves. Such areas as the control tower, static or mobile, and other essential operational assets are as much at risk from snipers as anything else, as are the technicians who man them.

areas full of highly trained professionals who are hard to replace, but they also house necessary machinery, tools, and repair jigs that are all vulnerable to high-velocity impact.

Accommodation blocks. If the staff cannot leave their barrack blocks for fear of being shot, this will seriously degrade the workers' morale and willingness to perform their daily tasks. With careful observation, the sniper teams will be able to identify pilot accommodation and transport, and so target the men and women who are required to fly the aircraft. Even the operation of unmanned aerial vehicles (UAVs) is not secure once the snipers find the ground-based controllers.

BELOW: The emergency services, whether on military establishments or civilian areas, are a key sniper target, since without them other attacks cannot be countered. If the sniper shoots a fireman and then starts fires, he will cause a lot of damage, and if he shoots anyone who tries to put the fires out he will soon deter other people from trying.

ABOVE: Airfield perimeters are far from secure against the sniper as he does not need to cross the fence or close in on the target. These groups of Russian paratroopers are embarking on a flight, oblivious to the fact that they are under observation.

Base vehicles. Because of the vast areas involved, vehicles of all types and sizes are vital to the running of the airfield on a daily basis. The loss of several of these vehicles, especially fuel tankers and aircraft tow vehicles, will lower the productivity of the staff and disrupt the normal daily routine. Snipers need to be fully conversant with all the types of vehicle and their role within the airfield framework in order to target those that will affect the airfield most when lost to rifle fire.

Control tower. An area of the airfield or airport that is often overlooked as a potential target for snipers is that of the systems used in the control of the surrounding airspace. Any control tower will be packed with electronics associated with controlling takeoffs and landings, and is therefore a viable attack option. Every airfield is likely to have a mobile back-up system, so this needs to be targeted at the same time, or as soon as it shows itself after the initial attack. At the perimeter of the field or close to the runway is usually the height-finding radar used to guide aircraft down in low cloud or darkness; damage to or destruction of this equipment can stop air operations. Also very prominent on most airfields is the main area intercept radar, with receivers, responders, dish, and gearing mechanism, and this too can be rendered inoperable by heavy-caliber sniper fire.

Emergency services. While not really being of such importance as to stop operations, the loss of the emergency fire tenders and staff will affect the morale of the pilots who have to contemplate landing without immediate support and rescue, and perhaps medical aid, especially if they know a sniper with a .50-caliber weapon is operating against their airfield and may be waiting on their final approach route.

Naval targets

The prospect of snipers having to engage, or indeed having to defend, naval targets has in the past been regarded almost with incredulity. But today all aspects of the military (and commerce) may fall within the remit of the sniper. At first glance it would appear incredible that a sniper could attack and have any chance of success against a large warship, with all its sophisticated technological weaponry and surveillance assets. However, his chances of success would rely not so much on divine intervention but on the sniper's overall knowledge and understanding of the target's capabilities and equipment, as well as its routine and staffing levels.

If the same problem had been presented to the sniper of World War II, he would have had little success against a warship above the level of killing crew members. The reason for this lies within the overall concept of warship design and weaponry of the time, rather than

ABOVE: Modern warships are not as heavily armored as their counterparts of World War II and as such rely on technology to provide their protection and firepower. This technology does not function well after hits from high-speed lead, and while in port or transiting narrow coastal waterways they become vulnerable to the sniper armed with a .50-caliber rifle. (U.S. Navy)

with his ability to consider a warship as a target. The biggest threat to the naval forces of the time was the aircraft, and to make warships survivable during an attack by enemy aircraft the designers had to provide the ships with the two things they needed the most, armor plate and multiple quick-firing guns.

Today, with warships armed with an abundance of highly accurate, quick-to-deploy missile systems that can locate, track, and engage enemy aircraft at extreme range, the need for a nest of quick-firing guns mounted upon a thick layer of armor plating

ABOVE: Shipboard personnel and their defensive weapons are very rarely at risk from anything other than missile impact. However, this changed with the terrorist attack on the USS *Cole*. Exposed crew can now expect to be engaged by snipers whenever they come within rifle range of the shore or fast sea craft in the world's shipping lanes. (*U.S. Navy*)

has become redundant in the minds of the designer and accountant, if not the sailor!

The modern warship is made of only limited thicknesses of metal, which means that the ship relies for protection on its weapons and the reduced weight of its bulk, which permits greater speed through the water. While this makes perfect sense, it does bring the warship into the target zones of attackers that would not ordinarily be considered a threat.

The role of the warship is to deploy to the open ocean and use its long-range weaponry to attack or defend, depending on its mission.

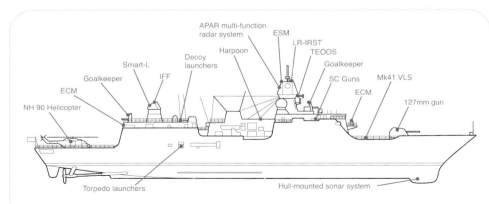

ABOVE: With an abundance of reference books, magazines, and DVDs highlighting all the major assets of today's warships it does not take too much research to identify areas of a ship that would render the ship inoperative or seriously reduce its operational capability if attacked by .50-caliber ammunition.

In this role the warship of the last ten years has excelled; the missile and radar have ruled supreme. Rarely has the aircraft got the upper hand of its waterborne adversary. However, during the Falklands conflict in the 1980s, the British had to move warships into inlets and harbors, drastically reducing the effectiveness of their radars and hence their missile defense systems. These were in effect coastal operations, an area we now see as being of increasing tactical importance.

The large and very effective radar-guided weapon systems of modern warships are designed to be effective out in the open ocean and away from large land masses. This removes the effect that land masses have on radar effectiveness, and hence missile reliability, against fast-moving and highly maneuverable aircraft targets that can be masked by interference due to the proximity of landfall. If there is a need to have warships close to land, however, and if we are seeing the beginning of the return to littoral warfare for naval forces, this brings with it a vulnerability

to weapon systems that would normally pose the warship no threat. The attack by terrorists on the U.S. Navy destroyer USS *Cole* in the harbor of Yemen on 12 October 2000 serves as an example of the susceptibility of the warship to seemingly small threats.

Naval forces as well as aircraft and land vehicles must now be added to the list of potential targets for the sniper, who should be instructed on such matters. The key to any attack against such a large and apparently unsinkable target by a man or men with small arms is a thorough knowledge of the ship's construction, layout, and capabilities. Such knowledge will allow the sniper to engage vital areas on a ship that may well be hidden from view and yet are highly likely to be vulnerable to high-speed small arms attack. For example, connecting just about everything throughout the ship is a mass of running cable, pipes, and hydraulic systems. Having identified where these are the sniper could do untold damage with precision fire. Knowledge of the ship's operations room, for example, an area packed with technology and key personnel, will allow for an attack that at least will hit valuable equipment or people, and at worst will cause damage to both the ship and the crew's morale. U.S. Navy warships are now fitted with Kevlar armor in sensitive areas, but this protective measure is expensive and out of reach of most of the world's cash-strapped navies.

With the sniper being able to deploy weapons ranging from .308-caliber (7.62mm) through to .50- or even 20mm-calibers, the skin of the average ship is only of limited protection, especially when taking into consideration the availability of armor-piercing, and armor-piercing incendiary or high-explosive ammunition.

To aid his attack prospects against a warship in port or otherwise close to shore, the sniper should also seek and be trained to identify and have a working knowledge of a ship's weapon and surveillance systems. This is the key to knowing what best to shoot at to impair the warship's ability to fight or deploy. The sniper may not be working alone, but may be employed to eliminate or limit a ship's ability to use its defensive systems for a period of time, and thereby allow other weapon systems to be used to sink the ship, such as aircraft that would otherwise be vulnerable to the ship's anti-aircraft missiles.

To highlight this, the radar can usually be found high up on the ship's superstructure. This might appear to be too large to be affected by a rifle bullet, but not so. The large paneled areas on radars are full of small and easily damaged computer boards that can be impaired by hits from a sniper's rifle projectiles. There are also running gear and cogs that enable the unit to rotate and therefore provide wide coverage; if the radar is stopped from rotating, it is stopped from working, and the system is useless!

Another target for the sniper is the ship's missile launcher. Most ship-mounted missile systems have an integral launcher that raises and allows the launch of the actual missile. The launcher is in essence a machine designed to lift the missile from below deck and point it either towards the target or just skyward. Some systems even have provision for a final information update to the missile via an IT interface located in their construction. There are many versions of such launchers, including some that have a number of missiles located on the launch rail at any one time, varying from single to multiple missiles. The launcher is usually constructed from the same thickness of metal as the ship or less, and so is vulnerable to attack from small arms fire. The latest vertical launch missiles in ready-to-fire cells are generally mounted in multiple missile groups on the main deck or on the deck below, and so are just as vulnerable to attack. With the whole missile launch capability housed in the one unit, any hit could inflict damage and reduce the weapon's reliability.

Vertical launch missile system

Vertical launch systems first appeared in fleet warships in the mid-1980s. They vary in size and can contain from over sixty missiles down to eight, as on the Canadian Halifax-class frigates.

Multiple and boxed missile launchers

Earlier missile systems employed various types of single, twin or boxed launchers. All are vulnerable to small arms attack, which is capable of rendering the missiles inoperative.

Knowledge of different types of ships and their roles, and identifying areas vulnerable to attack from small arms ammunition, will enable the sniper to plan which areas of the ship to target and the parts of a ship that, if impaired, will cause loss of capability, or may lead to additional damage and even the loss of the ship. To illustrate how accurate shot placement and the selection of the correct ammunition could cause seemingly disproportionate damage, consider the devastation that could occur if the ship's helicopter, or its aviation fuel tank, were hit by armor-piercing incendiary ammunition, especially if the hit was taken in harbor and when the crew were stood down. The potential result could be far above that expected and could lead to much greater consequences than ever planned.

As with most areas of target selection and tactics covered here it is vital to look at countering the sniper threat. These sniper tactics are already well known to the terrorist. It is the shortfall in military and police training that at present gives the terrorist the advantage. By considering the threat, it is possible also to illustrate the defense, and so truly provide counter-sniper options by providing proactive as opposed to reactive measures.

Ship design

The basic design and layout of a warship is very similar no matter who makes it or where it is made. Some navies are expressing a desire for their ships to be made to a modular construction design. This means that the ship's design allows technology progresses to be included into the basic hull without too much difficulty. In theory this keeps the ship current and in service longer, and allows the user to switch equipment and hence the ship's role quickly; the hull is multi-role, reducing the number of ships needed. What this also means is that the basic ship layout is the same across the navy, and allows the sniper to accurately predict where certain target areas are within the ship, and hence out of sight, in relation to visible references on the upper decks.

As with any design, from bicycle to warship, there are only so many ways of incorporating the essential components into a standard ship's hull. By studying the basic working parameters of a weapon system, you find that for it to operate on a rolling, pitching platform without its weight or operation affecting the ship's performance or balance, there are only so many different layouts that a design team can employ. This again aids the sniper in learning the general locations of the systems he would be interested in attacking.

In general, there are two types of internal layout of the surface warship—a central corridor with all the working areas leading off of it and hence closer to the outside hull, and a circular corridor with working areas inside its perimeter. The lower down you go into the hull, the more this may vary, but realistically anything lower than the water line is not likely to be affected by small arms fire, unless the sniper's plan is to use a multi-shot, semi-automatic weapon in the Barrett class to provide multiple puncture hits below the waterline, with the aim of slowing or stopping the ship while the crew struggle to find and plug the hull damage. The sniper is generally looking to engage weapons, equipment, and personnel on the upper decks or in easily identified areas down to the waterline.

Advances in warship weapon design have led to a trend to make them semi- or fully automated. This can allow for less manpower, and the more you remove the man, the more associated equipment is needed to make it work. In an automated gun for example, while the gun itself is in a compact turret with no visible outside assistance, under the decks is a mechanical system to bring the shells up to the gun, and below that a man to recharge the machine with shells when the ready rounds have been expended. All of this is pretty much untouchable by the sniper, but for the weapon to be automatic it has to have a locating and aiming system that replaces the men that used to do the job! If the sniper is trained to identify the associated parts of the complete system, then he can locate and therefore engage, with accurate rifle fire, the component parts that make the gun effective, i.e., the target-locating and the gun-aiming

BELOW: All radars mounted aboard ships are stabilized against the movement of the ship at sea and as such sit atop dampers and gearing that if impacted by high-speed, heavy-caliber rifle fire could fail to function and render the radar inoperable. Missiles are of no use if their intended target cannot be located. (*U.S. Navy*)

radars. As with the missile system, if you attack vital parts of the target acquisition and engagement process you can achieve results never considered possible.

While the role of the warship is to sail out of port and away from the threats that land poses, and into a scenario where its sensors and weapons put it at a huge advantage against any attacker, it therefore stands to reason that the sniper is most likely to engage a ship target while it is static in port or close into shore at navigational choke points. The static target will most likely be associated with a combined attack or a Special Forces type operation to reduce the enemy's capabilities, and therefore his deployment options. The other main tactic is to employ the sniper to attack a ship as it passes close to shore because of operational necessity or navigational restriction. An example of this would be entry or exit to port or through a geographical feature such as the Panama or Suez Canals, where a damaged or sinking ship would cause enormous problems and repercussions. Highly unlikely or ridiculous? Maybe, but just as unlikely or ridiculous as the possibility of the World Trade Center towers collapsing after aircraft impact. In the world of warfare or terrorism nothing can be discounted.

The terrorist attack

The suicide bombing of the USS *Cole* in Yemen in 2000 proved that a high profile attack on the mighty U.S. Navy could not only be carried out, but that it could succeed. In order to achieve this, terrorists must have carried out a detailed and lengthy study of U.S. Navy practices and procedures for warships that call into foreign ports for fuel, maintenance, or flag-waving visits.

The following scenario is presented to help understand how a similar assault could be mounted with a sniper option being selected as the main form of attack, and also therefore what counter-sniper measures could be undertaken.

Location: a Western nation naval port facility

Terrorists have identified that a member of the anti-terrorist allied force has a naval facility that is surrounded by civilian housing, shops, and shipping assets that will afford them a multitude of firing platforms. There is public access to the naval facility, because of historical ships and collections located there. The terrorists are therefore able to carry out a very detailed reconnaissance during their planning phase.

Reconnaissance: visual and research

The terrorists are able to rent an apartment that overlooks the harbor entrance and set about visiting all the port facilities, from museums through to harbor waterborne tours in order to gather information and to select the most appropriate target. They also scour all available literature on the potential target's assets and procedures in order to maximize the effect of their attack and achieve worldwide media coverage. Because of the West's "freedom of information" doctrine, and aided by the local newspapers' listings of all comings and goings from the port facility, they are able to select their target and plan their attack with alarming ease.

The target: a warship departing for a counter-terrorist allied fleet

The terrorists identify their target: a warship deploying on a six-month combined nation fleet tour. By studying cutaway diagrams found in several books and magazines (some provided helpfully by the target nation) the terrorists have identified areas of the ship that are vulnerable to .50-caliber sniper weapons. They have decided to use a semi-automatic rifle and will fire multiple armor-piercing flash incendiary and armor-piercing high-explosive ammuni-tion at the ship and crew as the warship transits the narrow exit from the harbor.

Preparation: attack and escape routes

Not all terrorists are suicide attackers. In this scenario the attack is to be carried out by snipers as the start of a campaign that will spread across the target nation, focusing on high profile military and civilian targets in order to cause massive disruption to both the victim nation's budget and worldwide status; so the sniper

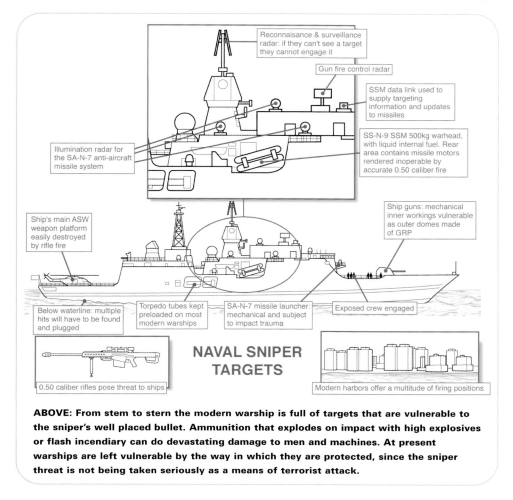

Reconnaisance & surveillance radar: if they can't see a target they cannot engage it

Gun fire control radar

SSM data link used to supply targeting information and updates to missiles

SS-N-9 SSM 500kg warhead, with liquid internal fuel. Rear area contains missile motors rendered inoperable by accurate 0.50 caliber fire

Illumination radar for the SA-N-7 anti-aircraft missile system

Ship guns: mechanical inner workings vulnerable as outer domes made of GRP

Ship's main ASW weapon platform easily destroyed by rifle fire

Below waterline: multiple hits will have to be found and plugged

Torpedo tubes kept preloaded on most modern warships

SA-N-7 missile launcher: mechanical and subject to impact trauma

Exposed crew engaged

NAVAL SNIPER TARGETS

0.50 caliber rifles pose threat to ships

Modern harbors offer a multitude of firing positions

ABOVE: From stem to stern the modern warship is full of targets that are vulnerable to the sniper's well placed bullet. Ammunition that explodes on impact with high explosives or flash incendiary can do devastating damage to men and machines. At present warships are left vulnerable by the way in which they are protected, since the sniper threat is not being taken seriously as a means of terrorist attack.

team must escape on completion of this attack. To that end a series of test routes will be trialed and tested in order to identify and select one, plus alternatives, bearing in mind the disruption they will cause. They will also identify probable weak areas of the local police and military response. The attackers will determine all likely approach routes of the police and military units, plus how long it may take such units to arrive at the scene. An escape

BELOW: All harbors and seaports are a veritable heaven for snipers planning to attack incoming or outgoing warships or civilian shipping. High-rise buildings near harbors, mean that locating a sniper attacking a ship would be all but impossible. (*U.S. Navy*)

route will be selected that will take the terrorists away from the scene and clear of any lock-down instigated by the target country's forces.

The attack: start point of a sniper campaign

After watching several warship departures, the terrorists know that the media will be in attendance, the narrow exit from the harbor will be lined with families and well-wishers, and the security will be restricted mainly to waterborne, lightly armed police, aiming to prevent small boats from getting too close and a repeat of the USS *Cole* incident. The security forces have not thought of or planned against a sniper attack.

The terrorist cell consists of a two-man firing unit with a .50-caliber sniper rifle, a two-man protection team with assault rifles, and two escape vehicles waiting out of sight in the apartment's underground car park, ready to take them to a safe house less than three miles from the firing point. Here they will lay low for a few days before individually making their way to their next targets.

As the ship approaches the harbor mouth the terrorist opens fire on the naval guard stood to attention on the deck, knowing that at less that a few hundred feet from the civilian crowds the impacts will be witnessed and panic will spread, to be conveniently recorded by the gathered media.

On board, the initial reaction will be confusion, and efforts to help the injured men. These valuable seconds will allow the terrorists to realign onto the areas of the ship identified from the books they have studied. To the rear of the ship, the helicopter deck and associated hangar become the focus for the snipers' weapon: the offset hangar door indicates the location of the helicopter missile and ammunition store, which backs onto the aviation fuel storage cell. Both of these areas are protected only by the ship's superstructure and have no armor plating—no defense against .50-caliber ammunition.

The impact of armor-piercing flash incendiary and high-explosive rounds are followed by an initial low intensity thud as the explosive force of the aviation fuel rips open the hangar and lower decks. Seconds later, flames and smoke escape out of the hangar and high into the sky above the now stricken warship. The final terrorist act is to fire multiple shots below the waterline throughout the length of the ship; while not being enough to sink it, this will cause an immediate problem and over-stretch an already stunned crew.

The attack takes less than ninety seconds before the sniper weapon is stripped and concealed in a hold-all, and the terrorists are on route to their cars and a safe house. Because of the surrounding high-rise apartments and shops, as well as harbor traffic and the associated echo, the firing point will not be located for several hours. Meanwhile the city will be brought to a standstill by follow up operations and the influx of media mobile units.

The world will see a powerful nation attacked in its home port, a warship at best too damaged to sail, at worst sunk across the harbor mouth, with dead sailors being pulled from the harbor. The world media will fail to highlight how difficult it would be to defend against this type of attack and would focus on the government's failure to prepare for this eventuality, providing the terrorists with the publicity they require to promote their recruitment and enhance the sympathy they desire.

Unrealistic? More fiction than fact? Not so. The abundance of literature and DVD footage available today, and the ease with which a detailed view of many of the Western world's military facilities can be attained, mean that this type of attack could be easily planned, if it has not been already. Until the world sits up and takes note of the sniper threat it will continue to be a possibility.

Large warships

It is essential for the sniper to have studied ship layout and design for all levels of shipping in order for him to be effective should the opportunity to engage such targets present itself. The overall size and construction of warships mean the chances of a sniper team doing any damage with anything less than a .50-caliber weapon are slim, but targeting of essential crew with smaller-caliber weapons is not out of the realm of possibility, especially with the ship's senior officers being easily identifiable while entering or leaving port. When targeting larger ships it is essential for the sniper to be able to identify important equipment and associated support systems, such as location radar and detection equipment. Well-placed shots into these areas can reduce a warship's ability to fight, leaving it vulnerable to other attack. The only real options here are attacks in port or when ships are close to shore, but the sniper must be able to engage such targets if they present themselves.

Littoral warships

The majority of smaller warships are constructed of lightweight materials including even glass-reinforced plastics, which means that small arms attack can cause serious damage if well placed. Included in this class of target are mine warfare ships, patrol boats, and landing craft, all of which have dedicated equipment and crews that can be targeted by snipers that are land-based, ship-mounted, or

BELOW: Day-to-day maintenance of warships' systems is carried out in port or even while anchored close inshore, with little thought of the vulnerability of the highly trained technicians who do it. Snipers have long harassed the technicians of the British Army working on communications masts in Northern Ireland. (*U.S. Navy*)

helicopter-borne. This was recently demonstrated by British Royal Marine snipers aboard a Lynx helicopter using an Accuracy International AW50 sniper rifle to engage the engines of a speeding drug-smuggling speedboat in order to disable the craft and allow boarding and arrest.

Specialist craft

Maritime Special Forces and other units all use small, highly agile boats to both deliver their men to shore and to also facilitate ship-boarding operations. These craft are lightweight and unable to take sustained or accurate small arms fire, and the crews and troops have limited if any protection from incoming fire. Ship-borne sniper teams or shore-based protection teams can cause devastation to attacking specialist units if they are expected or located in the approach to their intended target. Rigid inflatable boats (RIBs) carry their troops in very vulnerable positions and rely on speed and aggressive driving to protect them. This is only effective against lightly armed or untrained forces and is not effective against well-armed and determined resistance.

This was the case in the 1980s Falklands campaign when a RIB-based diversionary attack by the Special Air Service (SAS) in Stanley harbor, while the infantry attacked the surrounding mountain positions, nearly ended in disaster when the boats were illuminated by the searchlights of a moored Argentinean hospital ship. Since the Argentine ship was deemed to have carried out an illegal act, it was subsequently engaged by anti-aircraft artillery (AAA) and concentrated small arms fire from shore

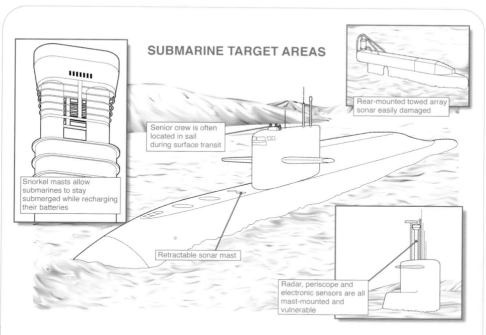

SUBMARINE TARGET AREAS

Rear-mounted towed array sonar easily damaged

Senior crew is often located in sail during surface transit

Snorkel masts allow submarines to stay submerged while recharging their batteries

Retractable sonar mast

Radar, periscope and electronic sensors are all mast-mounted and vulnerable

ABOVE: Submarines, also, are never associated with sniper attacks; this is a mistake. Submarines are festooned with vulnerable equipment such as trailing wire sonar and communications, as well as periscopes and radar masts, all of which are easily damaged by well placed shots that will render the boat out of action or at least the victim of a world wide media success for the terrorists, especially if the boat happens to be nuclear powered.

positions. But the SAS were forced to withdraw before all were killed as the boats took multiple hits and men were wounded. Snipers are a very real threat to small boat actions, one that is often overlooked.

Submarines

It is very unlikely that a sniper could achieve major damage to a modern submarine with anything less than a .50-caliber weapon targeted on any area other than the sail/conning tower or exterior control surfaces such as the rudder or dive planes. However, accurate fire against the submarine's mast-mounted sensors, from periscope through to search radar and the hull-mounted side-scan sonar, trailing-wire sonar mounting or other identifiable sensor mounts, could be easily achieved and greatly reduce the submarine's ability to detect threats and so protect itself. Mini-subs and swimmer delivery vehicles (as used by Special Forces and others) are very vulnerable to sniper fire when running on or close to the surface.

Target areas on warships

Most of the masts on modern surface warships are covered in sensors and electronics, curved, flat or just about any shape, and

RIGHT: This German coastal submarine passes close to shore every time it leaves or returns to harbor and the outrider RIBs are no protection against well placed terrorist sniper fire. Boats should utilize darkness to come and go from port, and not publish timings in local media.

all of these are potential targets for the sniper looking to cause damage, reduce a ship's effectiveness, or just be a nuisance to the enemy, so time spent on radar and sensor recognition is time well spent.

Radar. All surface warships today are festooned with different types of radar, varying from small, unobtrusive mounts through to large and obvious mast-mounted types. Whatever type they are, they are essential to the ship's ability to function and they do not work very well if hit by large-caliber ammunition. Radar systems are composed of electronics, circuit boards, wiring, hydraulics, framework, and gearing, and damage to any of these components will reduce if not eliminate the equipment's ability to operate, and so should feature high on a sniper's recognition training syllabus.

Almost all sea-based radar and sensor systems, whether for area search or fire control, have a hydraulic-based, self-stabilization platform in order for them to work by compensating for the movement of the ship. Any damage to this platform will also degrade the system's performance. Dome covers that are often seen as part of the radar structure are merely glass-reinforced plastics weather shields designed to protect the inner systems. These domes offer no protection against rifle fire of any caliber, and so a central shot on the dome will hit the system.

Weapon systems. To aid accuracy and speed of reaction, most of the weaponry on warships is automated and sensor-controlled. To identify and engage the controlling systems is to reduce or remove the weapon's ability to react in defense against an enemy attacker or offensively against a target. Most people realize that missile systems have associated radar that locates and guides the warship's missile to its target. However, most people do not realize that all but the smallest-caliber guns on board today's warships are also radar-controlled and -guided, and so are just as susceptible to small arms fire.

Most weapons systems have two radars or are of a combination type. One radar illuminates the target range for the weapon, and the second accurately determines the target height above the ground. So damage to or destruction of either radar will stop the weapon being used. For gun systems in Western warships, the associated control sensors are usually mounted on top of the gun itself and will look like a small radar; on Eastern and former Soviet systems the fire control sensors are usually mounted higher up on the ship's superstructure.

Missile systems come in two main types. Most of the older systems have a below-deck missile hangar and a mechanical launcher that raises the missile up from the hangar and supports the missile during the firing sequence. Newer systems have self-sealed missile units in a below-deck storage/launcher and fire vertically, so have no visible launcher. Both types are unarmored machines with circuits and moving parts, and are therefore vulnerable to impact from sniper ammunition.

Torpedo tubes. Most of the torpedo tubes fitted today are grouped in banks of three, on Western-designed ships, through to five or more on former Soviet designs. It is common practice for the tubes to be pre-loaded with torpedoes, since to save space the ships rarely carry, or indeed have the space for, reloads. The tubes are usually either glass-reinforced plastics or light steel in construction and offer no protection against small arms. This means that accurate rifle fire can damage the tubes enough to cause malfunction and a loss of torpedo firing ability. It is not beyond the realm of possibility to cause premature detonation of the torpedo warhead, with its associated explosive damage to the ship.

Helicopter and hangar. An increasing number of ships carry helicopters for anti-submarine and anti-surface warship action, so it is highly likely that there will be one available as a target for the sniper. Like all aircraft, helicopters are very easily damaged by small arms fire; any hit on the aircraft could remove it from operational service, thereby denying the ship of one of its main weapon and sensor platforms. The cockpit, rotor mechanism, body, and tail section will all offer targets on the usually exposed aircraft on the ship's deck. Even when inside the hangar the helicopter is still unprotected from armor-piercing ammunition. The aircraft hangars are normally located at the rear of the ship or slightly further forward, and one deck up from the main deck. Either way, the flight deck runs straight into the hangar to facilitate a short move to get the aircraft into shelter after it has shut down. The hangars are constructed with the same level of steel as the remainder of the ship, and so offer no protection against armor-piercing ammunition. As well as the aircraft and maintenance facility, the hangar also contains the aircraft weapons storage area and the aircraft fuel supply, in unarmored tanks. The impact of armor-piercing explosive or incendiary ammunition in this area will potential-

ly cause massive damage to the ship, with a high risk of internal fire, and so should focus high on the sniper's target list.

Decoy and electronic counter-measure systems. These systems are a combination of munitions launchers that fire decoys to distract incoming missiles through to electronic equipment that disrupts and confuses the sensors of the incoming aircraft or missiles. Identification of these systems and their targeting will reduce the ship's ability to defend itself or deploy into a hostile environment. Targeting should also include the decoys that are mounted at the rear of a warship and are towed behind the ship to confuse incoming torpedoes, thereby increasing the ship's vulnerability to submarines.

Night vision equipment. Just like their land-based counterparts, warships have large, easily

ABOVE: Warships are now deploying rigid inflatable boats (RIBs) with armed men aboard to ride shotgun and provide a cordon to reduce the risk of suicide boat attacks, but what is to prevent the RIB crew from becoming targets for the sniper? (U.S. Navy)

identifiable night vision optics, usually around the bridge, flight deck, and on weapon systems. These sights have very sensitive and large lenses, and are easily destroyed by rifle fire.

Ship's hull. An attack along the water line, or just below, with armor-piecing ammunition will puncture the hull and cause flooding, albeit not on a large scale. This type of attack is unlikely to sink the ship, but it will cause additional work and stress for the crew, who will have to find and plug the multiple holes caused by the sniper attack.

Submarine targets. Submarines are constructed to withstand vast pressures associated with deep water, and as such do not readily spring to mind as a sniper target. However, the submarine has many external areas that contain vital equipment and that are vulnerable to small arms ammunition. On modern submarines, recessed or raised sections along the side and on the bow of the submarine are normally passive sonar arrays that allow the sub to silently search the oceans for enemy submarines and ships. These systems are electronic and are therefore easily damaged by high-speed ammunition impact. Some of the systems are mounted on retractable masts that rise from the bow and stern decking and resemble thick posts. The submarine's sail or conning tower is a pressurized inner structure contained in a thin outer structure and so offers no protection for crew members who are targeted by the sniper as the sub transits in or out of harbor. Also located in the sail are mast-mounted sensors and optics. The periscope, both search and targeting radar, and other electronic sensors are all located in the sail, and therefore vulnerable to rifle fire. In addition, along the stern sides of the submarine, or mounted on the rudder, is tubing that houses towed array sonar for locating and decoying enemy warships and submarines; so to lose this through damage would reduce the submarine's ability to deploy.

Civilian environment targets

The increasing incidence of global terrorism has seen a rise of law enforcement sniper teams into a more prominent position. They have the optics to identify a suspect or target point, and the long-range ability to remain totally undetected by the suspect so that they can choose the moment of initiation without any warning to the suspect, and therefore perhaps prevent the firing of a weapon, detonation of a bomb or triggering of any other threat to the surrounding general public. To enable them to respond to any given threat or situation with the correct level of firepower there is a requirement for police sniper teams to have a selection of semi-automatic and bolt-action sniper rifles in various calibers at their disposal. These should include 5.56mm (.223-caliber), 7.62mm (.308-caliber), .338 Super Magnum, and .50-caliber weapons since there are situations that require the use of all of these types. Without them the snipers will find themselves making do with either over-powered or under-powered rifles, with the risk of injury to hostages or the general public, and possible consequential criminal proceedings against them.

Hostage situations

Police officers all over the world have to deal with hostage situations on an almost daily basis. This does not mean that terrorists take hostages daily, but that the police sniper is often called to a drugs- or alcohol-related domestic situation where one party has decided to take another hostage and threaten them with a weapon. These situations are normally ended by negotiation and nobody gets injured, but during all negotiations there is a sniper team positioned to provide real time intelligence and if necessary take the shot that will bring the incident to a close if innocent life is threatened.

Such incidents can take place in a built-up community where the distance to the

target can be as little as a few feet, or in open parkland where the distance can be out to a few hundred yards. A choice of weapons is essential. A .308-caliber weapon, for example, could carry an inherent threat of overkill, where the suspect is cleanly hit by the officer's shot, but the round has enough stored energy left to pass through the target and continue on to hit an innocent bystander or indeed the hostage. In such circumstances the smaller .223-caliber weapon might be a better option.

For police forces who have armed units deployed on vehicle mobile patrols awaiting redirection to incidents as they arise, a split of weapon calibers deployed would make sense,

ABOVE: The difference in size between 7.62mm/.308-caliber and the much larger .50-caliber round is evident here. When compared in this manner the effects of a hit from this larger caliber can start to be imagined. If you then consider that it can explode or burst into flames on impact then you get more of the idea!

with both types in each vehicle where budgets allow, or a .308-caliber team in one vehicle and a .223-caliber team in another. As the team works in pairs, a split of sniper and observer also provides for the selection of .308- and .223-caliber weapons within the pair, thereby easing the problem of weapon deployment.

Surveillance team overwatch

A sniper unit providing a protective overwatch for a surveillance team needs the flexibility offered by different caliber rifles. The surveillance team may have to move from close urbanization to a more rural environment in order to follow a target. Therefore the snipers may find themselves at varying ranges from the surveillance team, and thereby may need both short- and longer-range consistency of shot should they be called on for support.

Security protective cordon operations

Police sniper teams are also involved in protective cordon operations, perhaps for a visiting VIP or after an incident has occurred. Such operations may call for varying ranges to be covered and different types of barrier that may have to be fired through. When selecting the type, caliber, and combinations of weapons, the teams will have to carry out a detailed assessment of what is to be achieved in relation to any perceived threat. If they do not have a variety of rifles in their armory to select from, they will always be deploying with a "make-do" solution and a gap in their operational abilities.

Armed criminal incidents

The prospect of a failed or ill-timed bank robbery or armed heist turning into a hostage situation is an ever present one, so the police sniper teams need to be fully trained and prepared for a selection and control of stand-off positions from which they can overwatch and provide real time intelligence to the incident commander, and from where they can make the shot if required. Barrier penetration will almost always be a problem and deployment factor that snipers will have to take into account, as will the potential for over-penetration of selected ammunition. Police snipers must be given time to train and become accustomed to all the likely scenarios they will face. At present, few training facilities provide this type of flexibility.

Shot placement and anti-materiel sniping are often spoken of and listed in manuals as being in the sniper's domain, but it is very difficult to find any written instructions on these topics. This is an oversight on the part of many units, and an area that needs to be addressed if military and police snipers are to be used to their full potential.

Terrorist incidents

The worst case scenario for the law enforcement sniper team is that of a major terrorist incident. With law enforcement becoming the main line of defense for many countries, as their military forces attempt to keep the problem away from home shores with allied task force deployments, the possibility of police snipers having to be involved in terrorist incidents is becoming increasingly realistic. In such an incident, the sniper team's involvement will center around having to make a precision shot against a human or a mechanical target. Getting it wrong could invite a prison sentence.

Most police sniper team deployments will see them either in overwatch as a visible deterrent at times of heightened threat, or in an ambush position in an area of suspected terrorist operation as part of a combined

armed response and surveillance unit. This will pit the snipers in a more familiar role and one they should have trained for on many occasions. This role, while familiar, still comes with immense pressure, since almost invariably the shot will have to be taken in an urban area where the likelihood of general public presence is high. This and the fact that the police officers know they will face immediate suspension and an inquiry into their actions make for a very

ABOVE: British snipers train to operate in urban areas for operational deployment all over the world. Their experience in Northern Ireland has served them well and they have a vast level of knowledge of how to deploy in heavily urbanized scenarios. Here they train in how to deal with an IRA ambush.

stressful shot. Stress shooting training is an area that many in the sniper community advocate, and one that is becoming increasingly relevant. The sniper commander must spend serious time on devising realistic and relevant training scenarios for his officers, forcing them to both positively identify the target and then decide "shoot, no shoot" in a limited time frame. As with any training, these exercises must be followed by a detailed and frank debrief and discussion about the rights and wrongs of any given team response, to ensure that the officers leave with the right answer in their heads. There can be no gray areas. The time to make mistakes is in training, where loss of pride is the only result.

Hijacks

The threat of hijack is one that all police are well aware of, and most have experienced at some stage. While countries have a dedicated counter-hijack force, a local unit may be forced into an immediate response by terrorist action, so contingency plans should at least be considered.

Buildings. Incidents involving buildings are by far the most common area of for the police sniper, where they are likely to find themselves in the containment and intelligence-gathering role in support of the armed intervention team and negotiators. In this role they may well be responsible for either initiating the assault by distracting the target, or making a single/multiple target coordinated shot.

Moving vehicles. The police sniper must be prepared to engage moving or stationary vehicles, shooting through glass or bodywork, and so must have the caliber selections available to successfully carry out this type of engagement. They must also have the appropriate weaponry and training to engage and stop a multitude of vehicle types that could be used by the terrorist. These include automobiles, vans, buses, trucks, boats, and trains. The driver is always the obvious target when attempting to stop a moving vehicle, but this could result in the vehicle being out of control, so this option is often negated. Firing at the engine block, gearbox, and running gear are therefore better options, but only if the larger caliber sniper weapons are available.

Large shipping. A proven terrorist threat exists against both passenger-carrying and commercial shipping, so the police sniper must spend time familiarizing himself with all manner of shipping and be prepared to react and position themselves in order to cover, fire against, and provide real time intelligence on such targets.

Aircraft. Civilian aircraft, especially passenger-carrying types, have frequently been targets for terrorists. Police snipers have many previous examples to study in this field and should learn all they can about such incidents. However, they should keep their minds open to other scenarios and be prepared for different terrorist tactics to emerge. To prevent an aircraft from being moved or taking off, engines are an obvious target for police snipers, as is the cockpit area, but the snipers are more than likely going to be used as a distraction to allow for armed intervention after providing intelligence and a perimeter force.

Trains. Many train systems are extremely vulnerable to hijack by terrorist teams.

ABOVE: The everlasting image of the terrorist attacks on London in July 2005 will be the bus above ground, as opposed to the unseen subway bombings. The terrorist wants a visual worldwide media success and so this bus attack, while probably a mistake, actually served them well on the world stage. (*Peter Macdiarmid/epa/Corbis*)

There is still a sense of "it won't happen here," or even a total lack of understanding of terrorist intentions, such that security is sadly lacking in railroad operations. The terrorist attacks on London's public transport system in 2005 have all but been forgotten by most people who use the underground/metro trains and buses as they go about their daily routines. This allows terrorists to attack similar targets as long as they allow a suitable "forgetting" period.

The prospect of a hijacked train being used as a weapon by being driven head-on into a commuter railroad station at rush hour is horrific, but would be easier than might at first appear. Automated speed-restriction systems that disable out of control trains approaching end line stations can be bypassed by those who take the time to learn about the system. This information is freely available if you know where to look. Police snipers would be faced with the options of attempting to derail a packed commuter train, with the inherent loss of life, or allowing it to impact and hope the loss of life would be less. So is there another option? If time would allow, police sniper units armed with .50-caliber rifles could shoot at the moving train's engine and drive system at points along its route. This could disable the train and at least permit gravity to slow the train before it reached its destination. Far fetched? Maybe, but one option is better than no option and so it should be considered seriously.

Summary

The list of potential terrorist targets, and therefore the list of targets a police or military sniper should be aware of to obviate or to protect them from a sniper attack, would seem to be endless. But research and the time taken in compiling a target folder now should be dedicated, supported, and funded. To have any chance of deterring sniper attack, or stopping one in progress, the defending forces must take the threats seriously and plan to defeat them now. The frightening regularity with which insurgents use the sniper attack against troops in Iraq backs up my warning that such terrorist attacks are coming. There are various Internet sites (including Ogrish, Consumption Junction, and Prankboards) that show just how often U.S. and British servicemen and women are shot and killed by professional sniper attacks, and more importantly how each one is videoed and broadcast to heighten its terror effect on other troops in the area.

Terrorists are well aware of the success to be gained by dedicated use of sniper attacks, and it can only be a matter of time before they export this terror to the countries they so publicly identify as their enemies. During a period of three weeks in October 2002 ten people were killed and three others critically injured in sniper attacks in and around Washington, D.C. To allow other incidents like that, and worse, to occur by gambling that it won't happen again is not only foolish but downright irresponsible. Police and military forces should plan now to deter and stop such incidents before they do occur again.

CHAPTER 3 THE SNIPER IN URBAN AREAS

The likelihood of troops having to fight in urban environments is increasing. Many armies—especially those of France, Israel, Russia, the United Kingdom, and the United States—have experience of urban combat and have developed effective operational procedures to cope with this demanding environment. Such armed forces, with their experience of combating terrorists, have become proficient in operations where they are surrounded by civilian property, infrastructure and, of course, civilians. They have developed skills that have become vital in deployments to many different areas of the world on peacekeeping and internal security operations, with minimal warning. They have been able to adapt those skills and apply them to different situations, often, although not always, with demonstrable success. As would be expected, sniper teams have to operate in built-up areas as part of such normal deployments.

Urban operations bring with them a much tighter sphere of limitations, where a simple mistake can be seen and reported upon virtually instantaneously by the media, turning it into a major international problem within a matter of hours. To that end the

BELOW: To aid his concealment in urban environment a British sniper has improvised a gray and black urban suit from an issued set of Arctic white camouflage coveralls.

ABOVE: Baghdad, a mass of unconventional buildings around a maze of small roads and alleyways, is a hazardous area for any operational troops and is proving to be a sniper's kill zone for the Coalition forces trying to establish government.

LEFT: A sniper utilizes an improvised tripod to stabilize his shooting position while pulling back into the corners of a damaged building to reduce the chances of him being seen.

rules of engagement and the Standard Operating Procedures (SOPs) of an army must be carefully devised and then rigorously enforced by unit commanders, with ignorance on the part of individual soldiers being unacceptable.

The proximity of the civilian population greatly affects the way in which snipers can be deployed and used, and the safety of both the public and the snipers themselves must be given serious consideration. In certain situations the discovery of a covert sniper team by the local population may lead to no more than temporary embarrassment, some awkward questions, and possible relocation, but in others it could lead to the snipers losing their lives or suffering serious injury at the hands of an infuriated mob.

The main function for the sniper teams in urban operations is to use their covert techniques to remain undetected while gathering intelligence by using superior observation skills, providing overwatch to patrolling and other friendly forces, and eliminating threats as and when required.

Sniper operations in an urban environment

Perimeter force. Sniper teams have the ability to both see and reach out to greater distance than the normal infantry soldier, and, as such, they become the ideal tool to provide a perimeter protection force for a friendly or occupied urban area.

Route denial. The same skills also lend themselves to the role of route denial. The ability to engage the enemy at extreme range

ABOVE AND BELOW: All modern armies have access to specially constructed training villages in which to hone their warfare skills before deploying operationally. This one has served the British Army well for many years, helping snipers to perfect their ability to move around without being seen and to construct urban shooting positions.

while remaining unseen means that a correctly sited sniper team can control a series of roads, junctions or tracks.

Counter-sniping. Sniper teams should be positioned so as to reduce the enemy's options to deploy their own snipers against friendly forces, and seek to dominate all likely approach and firing positions before the enemy has an opportunity to locate and occupy them.

Gaps and obstacles. The most manpower-efficient way to overwatch gaps in defenses and obstacles, whether man-made or natural, is to deploy sniper teams to ensure that any enemy movement in these areas will be quickly identified so

BELOW: A British sniper deployed operationally in southern Iraq targets an insurgent preparing to fire a mortar at the British base area. The sniper's ability to both observe and shoot over long ranges has saved the lives of his fellow soldiers on more than one occasion.

that fire can be brought to bear on them.

Flank and rear area observation. The snipers' ability to observe over distance and locate seemingly invisible signs of the enemy make them useful in the protection of a friendly force or urban area on the vulnerable flanks and rear. These are traditionally the areas in which a force is most thinly spread and thus vulnerable to sudden enemy attack or infiltration, and snipers' observational and shooting skills can be used to overcome such threats.

Enemy observation positions. All but the most unsophisticated enemies will endeavor to deploy observation posts (OPs) in order to gather intelligence prior to attacking or commencing a guerrilla/terrorist operation. Such OPs will depend on the ability of the enemy troops involved to conceal and camouflage

themselves in order to avoid compromise and attack. Conversely, the ability of snipers to locate the enemy, however well concealed, will assist in the elimination of such potential intelligence assets of the enemy.

Locating and manning observation positions. Just as snipers are able to locate an enemy OP, so, too, are they suited to select and man friendly force OPs, utilizing their camouflage and observation skills. The unit reconnaissance troops and those of Special Forces are always going to be overcommitted and in short supply, and this makes the use of sniper teams even more desirable. The urban OP is the most demanding and difficult to occupy, especially if the local civilians are hostile to the sniper team.

Tasks set for such sniper teams will be varied and mission-intelligence-driven, but

ABOVE: The author in an overwatch sniper position in Kosovo, providing protection to the UN Police who were under an intelligence-led threat from organized crime in the Balkans. The vast amount of bomb-damaged buildings following the NATO air assault left the author and other snipers with a large selection of potential concealed firing positions.

RIGHT: The uneven layout and the amount of trapped shadow inside buildings provide the sniper with many choices from which to fire on enemy troops. This was one of the main reasons the sniper became such a weapon of choice in the Balkan conflicts of the 1990s.

ABOVE: The sniper will use all available assets to help in the reconnaissance of his intended area of operation before deployment. Here the author is overflying the derelict multi-story building in the left of the picture that he would eventually use for an operational deployment.

BELOW: The NATO air assaults in Kosovo left a lot of very visible damage. Any type of air attack will provide the sniper with more hides and OP locations than would normally be available.

ABOVE: Visible sniper positions have their purpose as here where their presence is intended to act as a deterrent to potential attackers during an overwatch of British Prime Minister Blair's visit to Pristina, Kosovo.

may include one or more of the following:

- Monitoring meetings
- Protecting friendly force patrols
- Locating and eliminating key enemy personnel
- Establishing area pattern of life
- Gaining intelligence on weapon and explosives movement
- Monitoring local reaction to on-going missions

Selection of likely OP positions is very demanding, since the lives of the military sniper team will depend upon careful selection, while compromising the operation is always a risk for the law-enforcement team. Therefore, any position selected, be it rural or urban, must meet the criteria set out in the mnemonic, COCOA:

C. Cover from view and fire

O. Observation of approach routes

C. Covered approach and exit routes

O. Observation arcs as wide as possible

A. Alternative positions

ABOVE: Prime Minister Tony Blair meets the crowd in Pristina, confident in the protection provided by British snipers manning all the local rooftops.

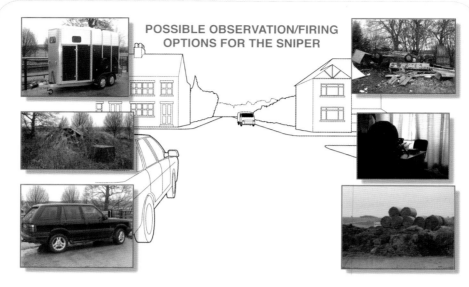

POSSIBLE OBSERVATION/FIRING
OPTIONS FOR THE SNIPER

ABOVE: The urban environment presents many concealment options for the imaginative sniper team, who may be in the place that nobody expects them to be, or where everybody looks but doesn't see.

When selecting a suitable location for an OP in a town or city in an internal security situation, the sniper commander must first identify his operational parameters. This will enable him to narrow his choice of potential positions that will allow him to meet his operational remit; he will then have to decide on a means of conducting a closer reconnaissance (recon) of each before making a final selection. The initial recon will have to be conducted in a way that conceals the reason for and location of interest from any watching locals, whether hostile or not; this can be a very difficult task.

How the security forces are perceived by the indigenous population will be a major influence on the operational 'choices. If the security forces and the local population are of the same or similar ethnicity the recon troops

may be able to adopt similar dress, mingle amongst them, and conduct a covert close-target inspection of the intended position or positions. If, however, this is not an option because the security forces and indigenous population are of differing ethnicity, then a much more elaborately planned recon may have to be mounted.

The close target reconnaissance team dressed to appear as locals may conduct their recon in various ways. Depending upon situational restrictions and local habits, a vehicle drive-past could be carried out, allowing a brief, external look at the target and surrounding area, while appearing to observers to be just another passing vehicle. It is very unlikely that more than one drive-past could be conducted without alerting the local population, so careful planning and preparation

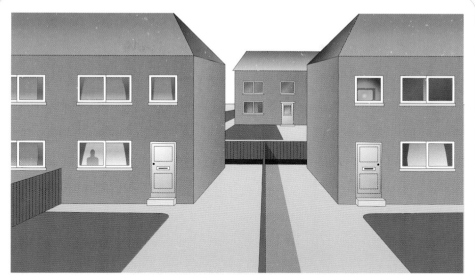

ABOVE: The sniper will be in the house deep in the background, shooting from a position of shadow and concealment, not in the front houses as indicated by the human outline in the foreground.

are essential to ensure that the maximum benefit is obtained. This will involve detailed study of the ground to be occupied, committing to memory the major points of the area, and being quite clear about the list of questions to be answered during the drive past.

Such a preliminary study will encompass all available intelligence and should include as many of the following aids as are available:
• Maps.
• Air photographs.
• Ground-level photographs.
• Tourist documents and local guidebooks.
• Archive TV footage.
• Local knowledge.
• Previous operational reports from the area.
• Face-to-face talks with troops or police who have worked there before.

Such careful attention to detail may enable a reconnaissance team to carry out a single pass of the intended OP position to glean a wealth of information and fill in gaps. There can be no substitute for such an actual visit to the site of interest, since matters such as daily routines, local awareness, and real-time changes are not covered in air photographs or maps.

The drive-past will involve the maximum use of peripheral vision and longer-range views. The team must avoid looking directly at the potential location, and, once past, turning for a second look, since either could well indicate to a watching local the area of interest and, in turn, alert the community. The composition of the vehicle crew is another factor to be borne in mind so that they will blend in with the local traffic; for example, if the majority of local traffic is made up of a single male, a male/female mix or a combination of old and young, a vehicle carrying four, young, well-built males will again risk drawing attention and thus compromising the operation.

The reconnaissance vehicle must be closely escorted by a back-up vehicle, and both must be in close communication, not only with each other, but also with helicopter- or vehicle-mounted support troops, who will be within a few minutes of the at-risk vehicle. This is a fundamental factor in every such operation; no sniper team should be deployed without mutual support.

After a drive-past, the team may well decide that further intelligence and local knowledge are required, and need to conduct a walk-past. This is a potentially even more dangerous operation, since it puts the snipers on foot amongst the local community, with only a personal weapon, usually a handgun, for protection, should they be attacked or cornered by a hostile crowd. Whether a foot reconnaissance is considered necessary will depend upon the situation and the importance of the mission. If sanctioned, it will be conducted with the same type and degree of intimate support as the drive-past.

As with the drive-past, it is important

BELOW: Snipers in a vehicle-mounted OP collect evidence against terrorists, and prepare to fire on them (should that be their mission) through a swing-aside panel.

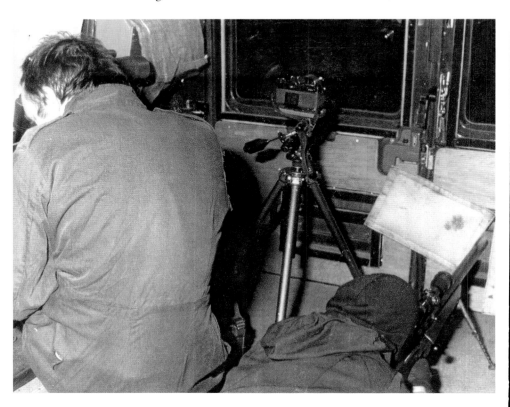

LEFT AND ABOVE: Improvisation of equipment has long been a factor for the sniper, from those produced by the camouflage factories of World War I through to today's snipers experimenting with urban camouflage. Here a British sniper instructor moves through urban rubble clothed in a homemade outfit made from an American desert night suit.

that the walk-by is conducted in an unassuming and low-profile manner, in order to avoid attracting local attention, with the snipers dressing and acting in conformity with local people and customs. The snipers will look for routes to and from the OP location, assess how difficult it will be to carry their weapons and equipment in and out, and decide whether they could be re-supplied or have to take in with them all the food and water needed for the duration of the operation.

The OP can be located in all manner of places, some worthy of consideration being:

• Derelict or unoccupied buildings.
• Rubble and garbage sites.
• Roof spaces above occupied houses.
• Bushes.
• Drainage systems.
• Abandoned vehicles.
• Closed shops.
• Schools.
• Churches.

The Close-Target Reconnaissance

Once the location has been provision-ally selected, a detailed Close-Target Reconnaissance (CTR) must be carried out in order to confirm its suitability and to validate that the sniper team's area of interest can actually be seen from this location. It is also necessary to confirm that the snipers will have a defendable location, should they have to fight from it. This entails a detailed and carefully planned covert reconnaissance, an operation that is undertaken by Special Forces, reconnaissance troops, and snipers in all theaters of war and on all military deployments.

Because of the sniper's ability to move around any type of real estate, be it rural or urban, and remain undetected by the enemy the task of getting in close to the enemy and

ABOVE: To the average observer this is no more than a derelict and abandoned car, but to a sniper it is a potential OP position.

Pre-CTR sources of planning information
Maps.
Air photographs.
Previous patrol reports.
Previous patrol commanders.
Local people.
Police.
Prisoners.
Captured documents.
Intelligence officer.
Electronic intelligence.
Signals intelligence.

CTR phases
Detailed planning.
The reconnaissance.
After-action report.

locating his strengths and weaknesses often falls to the sniper pair or teams. This dangerous task should be left to a force's unit recon platoon, if available; they are the true experts in this field, but more often than not it will be allocated to the sniper teams, as there are seldom enough recon teams to go round.

One of the snipers' first ports-of-call when planning any mission will be to the unit intelligence officer to gather any available information on the enemy and the target area. Sources of such information include after-action and patrol reports from any unit that has worked in the intended area, especially any other close-target recon reports.

The planning phase
As is to be expected, the CTR patrol is undertaken only after very detailed planning. Ideally, the sniper pair will team up with at least one other pair, but a CTR can, where

necessary, be carried out by a single pair, although this means that their ability to cover the target area is greatly reduced and the risks are substantially increased. There are many sources of information to research in order to assist in the planning of their task, and the level of the operation will, to a certain extent, determine how much is made available.

Maps. The pair will carry out a detailed study of the most up-to-date maps, looking at routes, obstacles (both man-made and natural), contours, the lie of the land, and distances.

Air photographs. The pair will also attempt to obtain either aircraft or satellite imagery of their target area in order to do a map-to-photo comparison. The reason for this is that a photograph will give a much more detailed and up-to-date image of the target area, showing such things as vegetation, signs of the enemy on the ground, and the overall area.

Previous patrol reports. Every military/police unit should, and usually does, keep patrol reports on file, and these can provide the planning commander with much useful knowledge even before he enters the area. These reports will have broken down the ground into detailed sections and give information on gradients, terrain and the going underfoot, as well as the location of civilians, and of animal life, both wild and domestic.

Ground-level photographs. Studying local photographs, whoever may have taken them, is an option not to be missed if it is at all possible.

Archive TV footage. The media have left few parts of the world unvisited, and it is very probable—especially if the operational area has been a trouble-spot before—that some TV footage may exist.

Tourist information. It may sound unlikely, but tourist videos, brochures, and postcards may contain vital images.

Local knowledge. Time should always be found to speak with friendly local people, if any, who may be able to provide information on local customs and behavior. Ideally, this should come from soldiers, police or government officials, but, even with them, care must still be taken to avoid compromising the forthcoming operation.

Time restrictions. The planning phase will have to consider the time available for planning, reconnaissance, and actually carrying out the mission.

Time of year. Certain times of the year may cause problems due to heightened public feeling. Examples include religious festivals, such as the end of the Ramadan fasting season in Muslim countries, the so-called "marching season" in Northern Ireland, national days, and so on. Such times should, if at all possible, be avoided, but if time and mission make this unavoidable, then the sniper teams must ensure that their drills and back-up force are well prepared.

Routes in and out. The team must identify not only a primary—and, if possible, a secondary—route into the target, but must also ensure that they have a good mental knowledge of the area in case they need to change direction once on the ground, and to also allow for different exit routes so as to avoid ambushes.

Local attitudes. The sniper reconnaissance team must be fully aware of local attitudes towards them, which may lead to a need to wear local dress or wear some form of over-clothing to disguise the uniform. But this is not the only factor, and the teams must also be able to emulate the locals' mannerisms and characteristics. Where this is not feasible, then the team must work out a suitable cover story for their presence in case of challenge from the locals.

Brevity reporting procedures
ALPHA—Building.
BRAVO—Male.
CHARLIE—Vehicle.
ECHO—Female.
FOXTROT—Moving on foot.
MOBILE—Moving in a vehicle.
COMPLETE—Inside.

Vehicle identification
S—Shape.
C—Color.
R—Registration (tag).
I—Identifying features.
M—Make/model.

Human identification
A—Age.
B—Build.
C—Clothing.
D—Distinguishing features.
E—Elevation (height).
G—Gait (how they walk).
H—Hair.

Specialist equipment. If entry is to be gained to a property, fence, gate or any form of building then the team will need to carry the appropriate tools to force or assist entry. Many Special Forces have a number of locksmith experts within their ranks, and these may be available if the mission warrants the inclusion of these troops. If the OP is to be more rural, looking into an urban area, then folding shovels or other construction tools may be required. The sniper team will invariably have photographic equipment, either digital camera or digital video, suitably doctored to enable infrared imagery since they will almost always carry out the target reconnaissance at night. Such equipment will enable images to be stored for use in the planning phase and is both quicker to use and more accurate than the old-fashioned way of drawing the image on paper.

Urban equipment list
Camera.
Food and water.
Dark cloth.
Tape.
Spotting scope.
Binoculars.
Glass cutter.
Report writing equipment.
Radio.
Hammer nails/crowbar.
Sniper rifle!

Orders and rehearsals
Once the plan has been made, the team will go through a detailed set of mission orders to

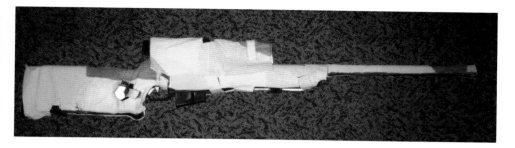

ABOVE: Sniper weapons need to be camouflaged too. This one has had a homemade cover applied in urban camouflage. Any cover must have provision for access to the working parts and the telescopic sight range and deflection turrets.

ensure that every person involved is totally familiar with all aspects of the operation. This is done to ensure that, whatever happens, the snipers and all others involved will react as one in any given circumstance. The whole team will then rehearse the major aspects of the mission, including actions to be carried out by all mission members on arrival at the target and also the actions to be carried out during major incidents or the most likely mission hold-ups or obstacles. These will include actions in situations such as hostile contact with the enemy, light in areas expected to be unlit, obstacles, whether predicted or unexpected, casualties within the patrol, either from enemy action or accidents, and what to do if one of the team becomes lost or separated from the other members of the patrol. The list of actions that will be covered will vary from mission to mission and this list is by no means exhaustive, but it is an essential task of any patrol to reduce the risk of loss of initiative should the patrol encounter difficulties.

The reconnaissance

The patrol itself will consist of several key phases, including the route in, actions at the final rendezvous (RV), the target reconnaissance itself, and the route out. The route in could be by vehicle to a drop-off point and then a walk in, or a completely foot route in. The snipers' immediate back-up force in the urban environment will most likely be vehicle-based, as this will allow them to be far enough away not to draw attention to themselves but close enough for them to react quickly should they be needed. If the target is close to the edge of an urban area then the back-up may be held at the final RV from the route in and react from there, if needed.

Urban reconnaissance differs from rural missions in that in the latter the patrol will work around the target recording all detail, while the former will almost certainly involve entry into some form of building that has been selected because its position will enable the sniper team to overwatch the target area, provide cover for friendly troops, or watch a target site or people. The point from which the OP is run should ideally be above the ground floor to avoid the chance of compromise by a nosey passer-by who looks through a window and notices something different or out of place. If the window is overlooked by other buildings, the room may need to be modified with a false wall, behind which the observation team can conceal themselves. This requirement will have to be noted during the reconnaissance phase. Such details as the color material needed and how it will be attached to the existing walls and ceiling without leaving tell-tale marks behind that will indicate the presence of a team if found at a later stage by the insurgents, will all have to be identified. Such considerations will not, of course, apply in an all-out war situation.

Once the target arc has been confirmed and all relevant information stored the team will extract themselves, leaving no sign of their presence, and will make their way to a pick-up point where they will link up with the remainder of their team before returning to base.

Types of urban area

The urban terrain can be neatly broken down into size-based categories and in general fit into one of four categories:

- Cities.
- Towns.
- Villages.
- Settlements or strips.

Cities. There is no one generally accepted definition of the word "city," while there are substantial differences in meaning between countries, for example, between the United States and the United Kingdom. For military purposes, a city is a large, densely populated, urban complex with a population ranging from about a hundred thousand to ten million. The needs of the city for manpower and the associated housing, produce, and all the other day-to-day items, coupled with concentrations of physical and electronic

BELOW: British snipers man an urban overwatch concealed position in the Balkans. By sitting back and using the shadow and reflective windows the team remain concealed for many hours a day over several operational deployments.

communications, result in a general tendency for ciities to expand ever outwards, absorbing adjoining towns and villages. One inevitable consequence is that, for the military, urban combat will continue to grow in importance.

Cities can be broken down, in general terms, into residential and industrial areas, each of which has its own characteristics. Residential areas are made up of small houses, usually with yards or gardens, and a road system that may be a grid in planned areas, or else simply a haphazard and sprawling network in the older European and Asian cities. These residential areas offer the sniper teams wide fields-of-view from selected positions, but also mean that movement is more difficult due to the larger

BELOW: British snipers in a rooftop location in southern Iraq provide mutual support to each other and the patrol in the streets below them.

areas that are potentially under wide-area surveillance by hostile elements. City residential areas may also contain high-rise buildings and business-type properties, such as warehouse and shopping complexes, and this type of terrain lends itself to sniper operations, although it also creates a mass of choke and ambush points that are all but impossible for the security forces to avoid. Industrial zones can vary in size, but normally consist of single- and multiple-story buildings with both flat and pitched (i.e., domed) roof sections.

Cities have many different routes for a sniper team to utilize, such as roads, streets, lanes, alleyways, railroad systems, and the often-forgotten below-ground systems, such as subways, drains, sewers, and tunnels. However, the enemy can use them just as easily as the security forces, if they are not covered or blocked. The closer to the city center, the denser the buildings and the

ABOVE: An urban area is a maze of movement options for the sniper, including sewers, cellars, underground walkways, and train lines that will all provide the sniper with ways of moving around unseen.

narrower the movement space becomes. Older street designs tend to be closer together and thus offer much reduced arcs of observation, while the newer style of high-rise buildings surrounded by open areas may appear more appealing to the urban dwellers and offer wider arcs of observation, and at the same time, conversely, making movement more difficult. The denser the population, the more pairs of eyes there are that can either compromise or assist the security forces, depending on where their sympathies lie.

Towns. These are no longer seen as a stand-alone urban area, as most have become feeder areas for the larger cities as the latter expand outwards. Towns can be broken down into the older type urban area that has evolved into a mixture of old and new buildings and structures, through to a town that has been planned and built from new, again usually to feed a larger city with workers and produce.

Villages. Village populations are usually below three thousand and tend to be away from the cities, and more in keeping with rural life and farmlands. The buildings tend to be the older style and spread out over a much more open type of layout.

Settlements and strips. These are areas that develop, sometimes spontaneously, outside previously occupied towns. They tend to be fairly new and, from the sniper's point of view, are open-plan in design. They will frequently develop into new towns in their own right, or become absorbed by an adjacent town.

Urban warfare characteristics

During an advance in a conventional war it may be possible to bypass a city, leaving the enemy garrison to wither on the vine and thus avoiding costly house-to-house warfare. But the advent of the global terrorist threat means that the urban sprawl is fast becoming the terrorists' preferred operational area. This means, perforce, that military and police forces have to train for manpower- and casualty-intensive operations in such areas. Over the past few decades U.S. forces have found that even a poorly armed, numerically much smaller, but nevertheless determined force can be a formidable adversary when located in an urban setting, as was the case in Mogadishu and Somalia and is currently the case in various cities in Iraq.

Many of the sniper's advantages are limited in the urban environment, so sniper teams must learn to identify and maximize those features that put them back into a position of advantage. Observation and target ranges are greatly reduced, so snipers must position themselves to control by denial and should establish multiple fall-back positions to allow for a much larger force pushing forward against them, and yet be able to continually wear them down through casualties and mental hardship.

BELOW: On a southern Iraqi rooftop a British sniper pair use a World War II Russian periscope to observe over the wall without exposing their position, and a "mouse hole" through which to fire the sniper rifle on direction from the observer.

Optical aids. For a sniper in the urban setting, to raise his head above a wall or peer around a corner can lead at the very least to discovery. This has led to a resurgence of interest in hand-held periscopes of the type originally developed for trench warfare in World War I.

Communications. Communications in urban operations also have to be given urgent consideration. The general make-up of urban areas degrades the effectiveness of many conventional military radio systems, and if the snipers are out of communication with their mutually supporting sniper team, or their indirect and direct support, they become very vulnerable to enemy action. A back-up system, be it cellphone, old-fashioned landline, alternate radio frequency, or, in the worst case, visual or hand-delivered messages, has to be considered and planned for, as do the necessary routes to be taken for either messengers or the sniper fall-back options. Such systems must be rehearsed if time allows.

BELOW: A British sniper utilizing both trapped shadow and his urban sniper camouflage suit to conceal himself from his enemy while he selects a target in his kill zone.

Ammunition. Urban fighting will invariably consume larger amounts of ammunition than an equivalent operation in a rural setting, and this will also have to be taken into account by the snipers. Urban operations produce fast, multiple, fleeting targets and, if sited correctly, the snipers will be presented with a target-rich environment; they must therefore have the ammunition to take advantage of such a situation.

Key points. These are the natural choke points (also known as defiles), such as narrow streets, crossroads, bridges, and tunnels, all of which can be made to work to the sniper's advantage if he is seeking to halt or slow an enemy advance. The attacking sniper uses his ability to out-think his enemy counterpart, and targets all key points as potential locations of the enemy sniper. In major buildings, the doors, alleyways, and entrance corridors also serve as choke points, albeit on a lesser scale, and can be used by the sniper with equal effect. The sniper must position himself to cover movement in roof areas too, since many attacking units train to gain entry via the roof and clear a building from the top down. Sniper teams on the roof will also have a wider field of view and fire, and with accurate use of their angle shooting skills snipers can cover both across and down into the street. They must, however, avoid the obvious and such prominent and easily isolated features as bell towers and church towers.

Obstacles. The snipers should identify all obstacles, whether man-made or natural, that may impede either their own or the enemy's

RIGHT: A British Army Chieftain tank of the Berlin Brigade in the British Army urban camouflage scheme used during the eighties in the Cold War. The author was so impressed with this design and its ability to conceal large armor he used it as a basis, along with others, as a camouflage pattern to conceal men.

movements. With skilled planning and use of defense stores such as barbed wire and mines, and deliberate destruction of bridges and buildings, the snipers can direct an unsuspecting enemy into a carefully planned killing area, and leave an obvious escape option that leads them into the next killing area, and so on.

Concealment. The urban environment offers a multitude of concealment choices for the sniper, and with careful reconnaissance he can make it virtually impossible for the enemy to locate him. Through making good use of adjoining buildings, roof spaces, alleyways, and gardens the sniper can move very quickly around his area of operations, enabling him to hit the enemy from several different angles. Such well directed shots from different directions increase the mental pressure on the enemy troops, reduce their morale and their willingness to fight, and, in the ultimate, may even result in a breakdown in command and control.

BELOW: The author's urban camouflage suit in the design stage. It is somewhat curious that after shelving the idea the British Army then issued a remarkably similar oversmock design to snipers for use in the urban scenario.

Camouflage. Disruptive pattern uniforms in use with the majority of armies are of little use in an urban setting. These designs are intended to emulate the non-straight-line composition of nature and have proved very effective in a rural setting, but urban scenes are made up of straight lines and require a totally different type of camouflage based on interlocking straight lines and with dominant colors appropriate to the city and country in question.

Natural effects like shadow should also be used to aid the snipers, while false screens and walls can provide concealed shooting positions that fool the memory. While the saying is "to fool the eye," it is actually the memory that is being fooled, because all the eye does is to show the memory an image for comparison with what it has stored, and if no match is found then the sniper will go unnoticed, making him, in effect, invisible. Camouflage is often linked with conceal-ment, but they are, in fact, separate skills: concealment is using an object to screen the sniper from the eye—and hence the memory—of the enemy, whereas camouflage is to be in full or partial view of the enemy and yet remain unseen through failure of the memory to recognize the sniper.

Deception. A carefully laid out deception plan can be a very effective way of fooling the enemy into exposing his strengths and weak-nesses, or to lead him into an area chosen by the sniper in which to kill him. The imagina-tion is the only limit to deception.

Building entry. The snipers will have to gain entry into buildings at some stage during an urban deployment. For this reason, crowbars, grappling hooks, ropes, and collapsible ladders are all to be considered as standard equipment for the urban sniper team. Knowledge of burglary techniques could come in very useful. Traditional metal drain-pipes and other architectural features can all be used by the sniper to gain access to upper floors, and such skills should be included in the sniper's continuation training programs.

Firing positions—prepared hides

As with any operational deployment, the sniper has to adapt his basic skills to facilitate the success of his mission. The selection of suitable fire positions is one such area where the sniper must use his ability to improvise and locate places that are not only suitable and tactically sound, but which will also confuse and intimidate his enemies by being where they will not think to look. There has to be a careful balance of the expected and the unexpected; either, alone, will quickly become the normal and pattern-forming, and this has but one outcome—failure.

The prepared hide is always the best option. This indicates that the sniper team has had the time and space to select and construct a suitable firing platform from which to observe and engage the enemy, in compliance with the mission statement and the rules of engagement. In this environment the snipers must ensure they are aware at all times of the sun and hence shadow and light reflection, and also of the effects of muzzle blast on dust and materials that may have been used to construct the hide. Dust is easily controlled by dampening down the area under the barrel with water or by laying a wet piece of cloth across the ground under the barrel and muzzle. The options open to the snipers depend on the buildings and urban design, tactics, and their own imagination, but some of the choices are as follows.

Room hide. The room hide is the easiest and fastest to identify. This is where the snipers select a room in a building, be it house, factory or high-rise, that will allow them to cover their arcs of fire, while remaining unseen. In the ideal situation the snipers will occupy a building that lies in depth to the first line of

buildings visible to the approaching enemy or the enemy under observation. The snipers will construct a shooting platform from available furniture, and also a defensive barrier for their own protection should they receive incoming enemy fire. This platform will be located back into the shadows of the room to avoid enemy optical penetration of the shooting aperture

BELOW: With the urban arena being made up of straight lines and different shades the sniper must camouflage his exposed skin in similar fashion. Here a British soldier is camouflaged to match his suit and surroundings.

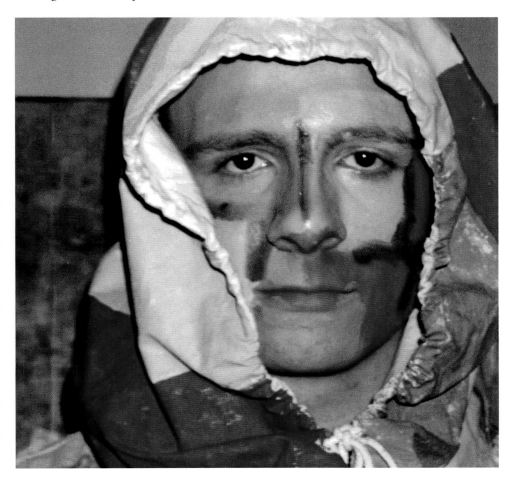

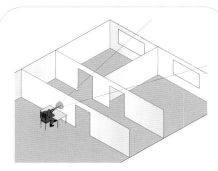

ABOVE: The sniper must locate himself as far back into a building as he can in order to reduce the risk of compromise. Where possible he should locate himself in a position where by holing inner walls he can gain arcs through the rooms in between him and the outer wall, and yet still be able to engage enemy targets.

and to maximize the effects of any trapped shadow. If necessary, the snipers will create shooting apertures by holing the internal walls to allow them to sit even further back in the room, or create a false wall using light material, which is color-matched to the walls of the room. The removal of window glass or drapes must match that of the surrounding area, otherwise it will become a target indicator for the enemy when scanning for possible hostile snipers. On the other hand, it is always wise to avoid shooting through a barrier. The sniper teams must also be aware of any windows to their rear and ensure that these do not silhouette them as they move around the hide. An important part of any room or building hide planning phase is to identify and practice escape routes from the room and from the building.

Attic hide. The attic of any house will provide ample room in which to construct a hide. All that is required to create a shooting and observation aperture is to remove or raise a roofing tile. But, in the same way that opening or removing window panes can be a target indicator, so too can be the raising or removal of a single tile, so a careful plan must be formulated to disguise this from the enemy. Due to the dark nature of the attic space, care must be taken to avoid the enemy locating any form of weapon flash, so engaging targets when they are moving parallel to or away from the firer will greatly enhance his chances of avoiding detection.

Floor crawl space hide. The space between the ceiling of one room and the floor of the room above it provide the sniper with a ready-made prone shooting position.

Roof hides. The use of the building roof can greatly increase the sniper's view and hence his field of fire, but, on the other hand, it will also increase the chances of discovery, since there will be inherently fewer objects and materials to camouflage the position effectively. Therefore the sniper must think of using such items as water tanks, roof-mounted small buildings, and air-conditioning plant, which will not only provide concealment, but will, in certain circumstances, allow him to shoot through or round objects and to sit back in depth, helping to defeat any enemy observation.

The sniper must be aware of the penetrative effects of both his own and the enemy's ammunition, and it will pay great dividends to allow snipers to test different types of building material such as brick, cement, and cinder block so that they can see for themselves the destructive power of high-velocity ammuni-

Firing position principles

Maximum use of available cover.

Good arcs of observation and fire.

Secure approach route.

Rehearsed alternative escape routes.

Defendable location.

Avoid patterns and the obvious.

Plan alternative positions.

Dominate your surroundings.

Height does not mean strength.

The higher you are the harder it is to secure your perimeter.

Mutual support.

Don't outstay your welcome!

If you miss, you move.

tion. The standard 7.62mm NATO round, for example, when fired at a range of two hundred and twenty yards, will penetrate:

• Three inches of concrete.
• Ten inches of loose sand.
• Fifty inches of wooden boards.
• Single stack brickwork.

Shooting through glass

In some situations the sniper may have to shoot through glass, in circumstances where either the firer is immediately behind a sheet of glass or the target is behind glass; both situations have their own characteristics. The bullet itself will be deflected upon impact with the glass, and the level of the deflection will depend upon several factors, including:

• Velocity and design of the bullet.
• Type of glass.
• Thickness of the glass.
• Angle of impact in comparison to the angle of the glass.

As a general rule, the bullet, irrespective of the angle of impact, will take the shortest route through the glass, so that the minimum deflection occurs when the bullet arrives at ninety degrees to the glass.

When firing from behind glass, as the

BELOW: The resulting hole from a 7.62mm/.308-caliber round fired from a USMC M40 A1 sniper rifle during through-glass testing at Quantico.

sniper may have to in the urban mission, snipers must be aware of the effects this will have on bullet deflection and the ultimate point of impact at the target end. The closer the weapon is to the glass, the less will be the deflection, but to be on the safe side it always pays to break the glass just prior to the sniper firing so as to allow a "free-from-barrier" shot to be taken. This can be achieved by the observer using his weapon to shoot it out or an implement to break the glass prior to the firing, or by two shooters carrying out a coordinated shoot where the first bullet to impact will clear the route for the second. However, both firers should adopt the same point of aim and be as close as possible to

each other's line of fire to maximize the chances of one of the rounds maintaining point-of-aim point-of-impact.

A major element in shooting through glass is the ability to recognize the type of glass in order to defeat it with minimal deflection. There are currently seven main types of glass the sniper may encounter in most urban areas:

- Laminated.
- Toughened.
- Wired safety.
- Lexan or plastics.
- Heat-strengthened.
- Float.
- Plastics film.

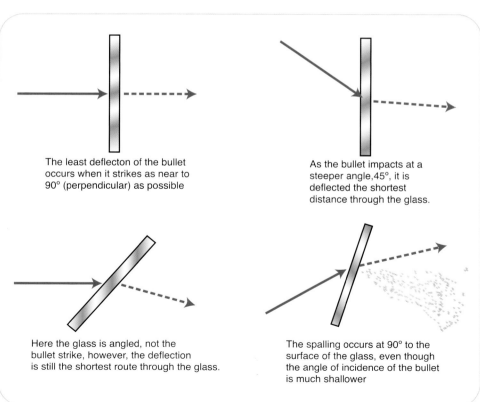

The least deflecton of the bullet occurs when it strikes as near to 90° (perpendicular) as possible

As the bullet impacts at a steeper angle,45°, it is deflected the shortest distance through the glass.

Here the glass is angled, not the bullet strike, however, the deflection is still the shortest route through the glass.

The spalling occurs at 90° to the surface of the glass, even though the angle of incidence of the bullet is much shallower

Laminated. Laminated glass is the most commonly used type of glass in business and retail buildings, and is also used for windscreens in automobiles, buses, and trucks. It comprises several layers of float glass bonded together with transparent plastic films that serve to hold the glass together when it is broken.

Toughened. Toughened glass (also known as safety glass) is produced by applying a special treatment to ordinary float glass after it has been cut to size and finished; it is then heated to about 620 degrees Centigrade and then rapidly cooled. The result is a glass that, if broken, splits into small pieces (beads) without sharp edges. It is very popular where glass walls or large weight-bearing glass panels are required, for example, in large commercial offices and shopping malls. It is also manufactured in tinted shades, which is popular for use in offices, particularly in the lower levels, and automobile windows.

Wire safety. This is float glass that has been strengthened during manufacture by the addition of steel wires through the inner glass. It is one of the oldest types of strengthened glass.

Lexan or plastics. Lexan polycarbonate is strictly speaking not a glass, but it is used in places often associated with glass, such as bus shelters. It is generally tough, has excellent clarity and light transmission properties, and is a good fire retardant, but it is nowhere near as strong as glass.

Heat-strengthened. While not common, heat-strengthened glass may be encountered by the sniper. It is produced by a less rigorous heating process than safety glass and has only half the resultant strength, which means that it breaks into larger shards when broken.

Float. This could be called the basis of all other glass and is formed by pouring molten glass over a bed of molten tin, resulting in a perfectly flat glass sheet with excellent light transmission properties but low physical strength. It is the type most commonly found in residential buildings and everyday uses. It can be either single- or, as is more common today, double-layered (glazed) and is generally 4mm in thickness. Like heat-strengthened glass, it breaks into large sections or shards when broken.

Plastics film. This is float glass with an additional layer of plastics film, which is applied to reduce the hazard if the sheet is broken; it is more of an upgrade than a discrete type of glass. It is a cheap method of providing some form of protection from flying glass after a terrorist bomb incident.

Bullet deflection

No matter which type of glass the sniper fires through, there will always be a degree of deflection of the bullet from its original flight path, and to ignore this is to risk missing the target, an option that just is not acceptable to today's police and counter-terrorist sniper. As with any type of barrier, various factors affect this deflection to a greater or lesser degree, and all of these must be taken into account by the sniper before shooting, wherever time

permits. The factors are:
- Bullet type and design.
- Glass type.
- Number of layers.
- Range.
- Distance from glass to the target.
- Angle of impact of the bullet to the glass angle.

A shooting angle as close as possible to a ninety-degree angle of impact should always be sought, since this leads to less deflection. The bullet will be deflected to take the shortest route through the glass width, and so the angle of the glass will influence the deflection degree of the bullet.

Another factor to consider is the break-up of the bullet as it impacts the glass surface, which varies according to the type of glass and thickness, as well as the composition of the bullet. Generally, the bullet core and jacket become separated and the core then fragments, becoming a mini-shotgun round as it continues along its trajectory.

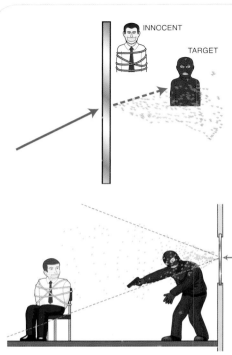

ABOVE: With a hostage outside the expected spalling hazard area the sniper can use spalling and secondary missile hazard to the impact trauma suffered by the intended target.

Spalling. These core fragments are accompanied on their path by the broken glass, which forms a secondary, if lesser, missile hazard known as "spalling," The following basic principles apply:
- The glass fragments travel in a cone shape from the bullet entry point outwards.
- The farther away from the sheet of glass, the wider the cone.
- The closer to the glass sheet, the greater the chance of injury from flying glass.
- The glass cone will travel approximately ninety degrees to the angle of the glass, irrespective of the bullet incidence.
- Injury is unlikely beyond about six feet from the sheet of glass.
- Particles from a sheet of toughened glass are more likely to cause injury due to their large size.
- Laminated glass is less likely to injure due to the inter-layer bonding.

Escape and evasion
The bottom line in any survival scenario is the desire to stay alive, which requires the following characteristics:
- Self-discipline.
- Physical fitness.
- Self-confidence.
- Sense of humor.

ABOVE LEFT: The bullet will take the shortest path through the glass which will deflect it off its original path in all but a 90-degree impact. The glass spalling will always fly away from the glass at a 90-degree angle.

ABOVE: Here the sniper has to make the choice of firing and risking injury to the hostage from flying glass, or not firing and the hostage being killed by the terrorist.

Of these, self-discipline is the overriding factor, since this allows the survivor to control and assess all that is going on around him and to work out the best options within the given situation, bearing in mind the available kit and equipment. It is thus essential that the instant the sniper finds himself on the run, he must find a place of immediate refuge that ideally will allow him to conduct a brief stocktaking of his position and equipment. The level of rations, water, and weaponry, coupled with any personal injury, and what is known of the enemy situation will allow the survivor to carry out a quick battle appreciation and formulate a

plan. Without a plan, the sniper is just another civilian stumbling towards the certainty of capture and perhaps death.

Any escape and evasion plan must sooner or later involve movement towards friendly forces. Wherever possible the escaper should move at night, although it must never be forgotten that the enemy will have night viewing optics. Ideally, the route should be broken down into logical bounds or distances with easily identifiable reference points to aid directional accuracy. Roads and tracks should be avoided, unless there is no option other than to traverse a large urban area, where boldness may actually help, since sometimes the best place to hide is right out in the open. In general, however, the escaper must leave the urban area as soon as possible and skirt it, utilizing its light and reference points, while remaining in the shadows. The normal pitfalls of sky lining, muddy and crop areas must be avoided since highly visible ground signs will be left. The escaper should also avoid contact with humans wherever possible and never display aggressive behavior.

Movement by day should be avoided as much as possible, although sometime this may not be an option and the escaper may have to make the best of a bad situation, which is where confidence and a good sense of humor can help him cope with the stress and pressure. If daylight movement is unavoidable then the opportunity should be seized with both hands and the escaper should be bold, hiding in the open, using any available aid such as bicycles, trains, or boats with every apparent confidence. Curiously, animals and small children are a major danger in the urban area, since they both seem to have some sixth sense that enables them to single out someone acting out of character and have no hesitation in bringing it—usually loudly—to someone's attention! In essence, escape depends on the strongest possible desire to survive, good luck, and good training.

Thermal threats

The advent of thermal cameras and optical sights has added yet another factor for sniper teams to consider. Various civilian companies have entered the equipment market with solutions of differing complexity. A more traditional method—which is both very simple and cheap—is a modification of a German sniper camouflage method from World War II, in which the sniper constructs an umbrella-type screen to which he then adds fresh local foliage. This has been proven to conceal the sniper from both visual and thermal detection.

At the other end of the scale, many very technical efforts are being made to provide soldiers with a defense against thermal optics, and one that has had considerable success is the thermal protection suit made by a British company named ROTEC, which gives protection against near infrared and thermal threats. This consists of an oversuit (trousers, smock, gloves, hood, face mask, and glasses) that rolls up to fit into a small stuff-sack, comparable in size to a lightweight sleeping bag, and takes up comparatively little room in a rucksack. The outfit also allows the wearer complete freedom of movement and does not interfere with his senses, such as sight and sound. The suit is made from a special material that can be supplied in any current camouflage pattern, can accept additional natural camouflage, and has low water retention properties. Specifications are as follows:

- Effective camouflage in ultra violet, visual, near- and far-infrared spectra.
- Lightweight—complete suit less than 4½ pounds.
- Low bulk.
- Rustle free.
- Low water retention.
- No sensory interference.
- Compatible with helmets, load-carrying equipment, and body armor.
- Available in many different camouflage patterns.

Sniper-control systems

In urban operations, more than any other, sniper teams have to be certain of their target and in a terrorist or criminal scenario the actual identity of a potential target may have to be verified. For this reason several companies have now produced sniper-control systems that allow the sniper controller or commander to see exactly what the snipers under his command can see via miniature cameras attached to the snipers' weapon sights. These systems are becoming a "must-have" item for law enforcement and counter-terrorist forces, and are starting to appear in military circles as well, with CastFire Solutions producing one of the newer systems on the market.

The KAPPA CVS-RS miniature telescopic sight camera system. It was originally designed at the request of the German Special Forces and is a prismatic splitting system that is designed to interface with any rifle telescopic

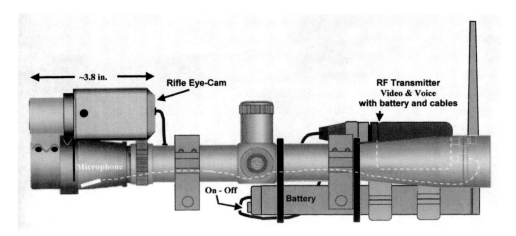

ABOVE AND BELOW: Often a sniper in military and law enforcement services needs confirmation from his controller/commander that his target is "legitimate." This CastFire Solutions Rifle Eye-Cams system can be mounted on the sniper rifle and contains a video and voice transmitter that allows the commander to see exactly what the sniper sees so that instructions (such as permission to shoot) can be given and recorded. Particularly in law enforcement circumstances, criminal proceedings could be taken against the sniper and/or his controller if they get it wrong.

sight. A secure radio link transmits the image to a base station where it is shown on a split screen TV monitor, allowing clear images of the sniper's arcs to be seen by the operational commander. The system transmits via a small, belt-mounted transmitter worn by the sniper and can be linked to either additional base stations or air assets, such as a helicopter or command aircraft. The system does not interfere with the sniper's sight and is available in either color or black-and-white versions. The system can be coupled to either a hard-drive or a video link to provide legal evidence or debrief material for use in the training environment. The system's main characteristics are:

131

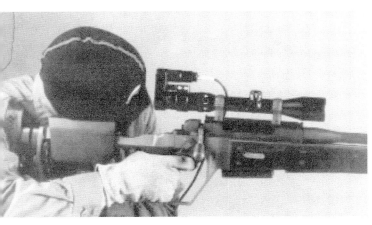

LEFT: The **KAPPA CVS-RS** is a miniaturized riflescope camera system for law enforcement marksmen and military snipers that transmits and records images from riflescopes exactly the way they are perceived by the firer. The images can later be analyzed in detail in slow motion.

- High resolution image.
- Video image with no interference to the sniper.
- Easy adaptation to many telescopic sights.
- Color or black-and-white image.
- Image transfer by either wire or radio.
- Compact and lightweight.
- Automatic brightness controls.
- Latest visualization technology.
- Video documentation.

Russian snipers

In World War II the Russian snipers built a fearsome reputation, with the defense of Stalingrad producing one of the most successful snipers in history, Vassili Zaitsev. This skills base was lost, however (as also happened in the West), when the Soviet Army developed its Cold War strategy of fast-moving, deep-penetration armored thrusts in which there was no place for a sniper. He was replaced by a section marksman, who was included in the basic formation of the infantry platoon. This decision would return to haunt them when they deployed to Chechnya in 1991, when a lack of snipers left them exposed and vulnerable.

New marksmen were trained on the Dragunov SVD semi-automatic sniper rifle and were given regimental-level training by a designated officer, who instructed them in such skills as marksmanship and target selection. These courses focused on developing a highly competent shooter, but did not produce the forward-thinking, multi-talented sniper of old. The Russian action in Afghanistan illustrated this as the marksmen were found to be wholly inadequate, and the Russians were forced to revisit their training policy, leading to the restoration of army-level sniper training.

LEFT: The proliferation of the Soviet-era Dragunov or SVD sniper rifle means that it will be encountered all over the world in the hands of terrorists. It is an accurate and comfortable rifle to use, and one that is currently doing a lot of damage to U.S. and British troops in Iraq.

Urban advice for snipers

Avoid daytime movement.

Avoid windows when moving inside buildings.

Identify dominant colors for camouflage.

Utilize depth inside buildings and shadow.

Don't open windows that are not open.

Don't be the only open window on the street.

Use screens to conceal and reduce risk of silhouetting.

Avoid ground floors.

Blend in with surroundings if covert.

Avoid obvious clothing and weapons if overt.

Ensure you have a proven escape route.

Last-ditch survival

There are many different fighting skills that a person can learn, such as the various types of karate or judo, all of which provide useful methods of self-defense or of disabling an attacker. Those arts, however, require years of dedicated learning and practice, time that the military sniper does not have. Of course, the sniper should seldom—preferably never—find himself in a life-or-death, hand-to-hand struggle with an opponent; his skill at remaining concealed should preclude involvement in such dramas. The preferred option is to walk quietly away and live to fight another day.

As with true survival skills, the sniper requires no more than the very basic skills and knowledge of fighting at extremely close quarters. The aim should be to achieve a standard slightly higher than that of the average civilian, so that the sniper is able to defend himself well enough to avoid serious injury and to get away.

Conclusion

Urban conflict will grow in importance as the population in almost every country gravitates towards the cities, a problem for the military that is exacerbated by the ever-present and increasingly demanding media. Using the latest communications technology, reporters can broadcast battlefield images to the world, often reaching their global audience before the commander on the ground has received his own action reports. Except, perhaps, in the case of the U.S., Russian, and Israeli armies, the days are long gone when a stubborn enemy entrenched in an urban setting could be removed by massive firepower. As a result, soldiers will have to enter every building and painfully remove the enemy one at a time, with the associated casualties inevitably associated with such tactics.

The sniper has worked in an urban environment for many decades and has a clear role in such warfare. He can dominate an area and provide overwatch protection to those who must, by the very nature of their task, expose themselves to the enemy's fire; for example, vehicle check-point teams and overt patrols. Thus, an understanding of how snipers work is essential to the soldiers who now have to operate either under the threat from hostile snipers or under the watchful protection of their own, as happens now on a daily basis in such places as Baghdad and Basra.

ABOVE: Snipers must maintain training in last-ditch defense by unarmed combat. The worse case scenario of being caught with an enemy in a building or indeed anywhere at close quarters will entail a physical struggle to remain alive, and snipers must know how to attack and kill with their bare hands if necessary.

CHAPTER 4

THE SNIPER IN MOUNTAIN AREAS

The role of the sniper is one that demands constant training and the mastery of new skills. He has to be able to operate in any environment and at any time in order to support his parent unit. Mountainous regions are as likely a setting for the sniper's skills as any other, but in this demanding arena the sniper will find that previously learned skills that have carried him through normal combat are no longer quite enough. As a result, he will have to master the skills of survival in the mountains under both summer and winter conditions, and learn how the change of terrain, altitude, and vegetation will affect his ability to operate, shoot, and remain unseen.

Before he can even think of employing his unique skills in such a physically and mentally demanding environment the sniper has to master the basics of mountain warfare. This entails learning skills such as climbing, navigation, survival, and skiing, and calls for high levels of physical endurance. For the mountain soldier every piece of equipment, food, and water must be carried on his person. The sniper must not only carry the same basic load as everyone else in the unit, but must also carry his sniping weapon, his special ammunition, and the associated equipment.

ABOVE: German mountain warfare snipers in the Austrian Alps engage targets along the valley and up into the mountains as part of their build-up training prior to moving into the higher mountains.

Climbing and Rope Skills

The very fact that the sniper will be working in mountainous terrain means that he must be confident in the use of ropes, carabiners, and climbing harnesses to facilitate his movement. This entails attending special high-altitude sniping courses, but only after he has already passed both the basic sniping and the normal infantry mountain warfare courses.

ABOVE: A German mountain sniper undergoes one of the course entrance tests, which cover every aspect from rope knots though to this deep ravine rope cross with full equipment. Not a trip for the faint hearted.

The German Army sniping-at-altitude course at Mittenwald in Bavaria, on the German/Austrian border is typical and lasts ten days:

- **Day 1.** Opening address; equipment issue; climbing revision; navigation exercise; climbing/rappelling/traverse test.
- **Day 2.** Angle-shooting lecture; foot move to 5,750 feet; angle-shooting fire-position practice; preparation for move to Austria.
- **Day 3.** Move to Austria; range work with pistol/rifle/40mm grenade launcher; first aid training.
- **Day 4.** Range work, four hundred to a thousand yards; mountain navigation lecture; night range work.
- **Day 5.** Range work; uphill shooting; sports afternoon; mountain warfare lecture.
- **Day 6.** Alpine training; forced march; climbing exercise; rappelling; observation test; written test.
- **Day 7.** Range work; downhill shooting; downhill night shooting using illumination; overnight bivouac in mountains.
- **Day 8.** Range work; downhill shooting.
- **Day 9.** Downhill shooting test; return to Mittenwald.
- **Day 10.** Debrief and disperse.

LEFT: A German mountain trooper prepares a sniper position high up in the mountains. With a long drop to the valley below after a slide of around 400 yards of scree, he takes care to ensure that he has some form of safety at his rear while working.

CLOTHING AND EQUIPMENT

Basic uniform

The basic issued uniform of most armies is rarely adequate for mountain warfare, so the high-altitude sniper must usually take steps to supplement his uniform with extra items. The start point is, of course, a good, hard-wearing basic camouflage uniform, and the German Army has a particularly good example, being sturdy and longlasting. With today's materials and fabrics, it is possible to have a strong and yet not too bulky uniform with added protection of windproof and waterproof garments made from materials such as Gore-tex to go over the basic uniform. This will add to the layered defense against the elements, but without a huge increase in the weight of the equipment that must be carried. There will, of course, always have to be a compromise between the ideal and the additional weight, and this will be a continuing process, as new equipment and materials become available.

Underwear is also of extra importance as the principle of the layer system for fending off the cold is a sound one, and good thermal

BELOW: It is wise to familiarize yourself with a potential enemy's equipment. Here a table is laid out with all the sniper equipment used by Russian mountain snipers. This equipment saw good service in the mountains of Afghanistan and Chechnya.

underwear is an essential component. Nor is just one type of underwear sufficient, since normal underwear is also needed for moving any distance under summer conditions, as the movement induces excess sweating. Under such conditions, if a thermal lining is

ABOVE: The angle of the heads gives some idea of what lies ahead that day for the men on this mountain sniper course. The course is almost entirely up in the mountains and is focused on foot and arm power!

being worn this will lead, first, to discomfort and, eventually, if the warning signs are not heeded, to soreness and heat injury. A layer of quilted or insulated clothing should also be available for wear in extremely low temperatures, and must be of a design that will fit under normal clothing without unduly restricting body movement.

LEFT: The German Army issues all its sniper teams with the Accuracy International G22 sniper rifle and a set of laser rangefinding binoculars to assist in the accurate judging of distance to the target. This greatly improves first round hits and allows the snipers to be very effective in this harsh terrain.

ABOVE: When you look at the mountain paths in the distance from these German mountain troops you can start to see the damage a well-placed sniper team could do to troops trying to advance along the exposed route.

Footwear. For the mountain sniper, good socks and boots are absolutely essential, because not only does he have to walk long distances with heavy loads, but he also has to climb and ski in them. Again, the German Army has good equipment in the Lowa boot, although the British Pro boot is also a good choice. A good tread pattern on the boots is even more important than in the lowlands, because a loss of footing in the mountains is not just a stumble but could lead very quickly to injury or death.

Gloves or mittens. The hands are of vital importance to the sniper, so under mountain conditions he must ensure he has adequate protection from both the cold and from the harsh environment in which he will work, while still being able to operate his rifle correctly. One example is the British Army Combat 95 clothing, which includes two sets of gloves. The inner, or contact glove, is made of thin, stretchable material with, impregnated into the palms, a multitude of hard-wearing blisters that assist in grip. The outer glove is made of leather with a Gore-tex/Pertex lining to provide maximum protection and warmth.

Headgear. The provision of suitable headgear is also important for snipers. The main factor they must remember is camouflage; anything that will attract an enemy's

141

attention must be avoided at all costs. There is little to be gained—and possibly a life to be lost—if a sniper wears an expensive camouflaged uniform, only to give his presence away by a colored patch on his cap, or a large pair of goggles with a very characteristically shaped, jet-black, shiny facepiece.

RIGHT: German snipers scan the mountains for signs of potential targets or movement. One uses the issued laser rangefinders; the other has cut his oversuit in an attempt to add depth and contour to his personal camouflage.

BELOW: Climbing to the final fire position is physically demanding in the Alps, and the snipers must carry climbing equipment as well as their normal sniper gear. Here students climb up into their intended firing position ready to engage targets in the valley below.

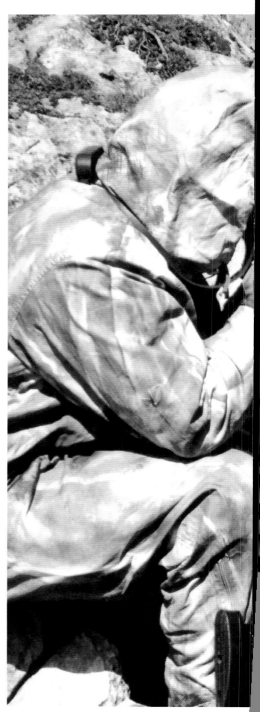

ABOVE: A German sniper wearing the self-made oversuit used for concealment in the rock areas high up in the mountains. It is merely the snow oversuit spray-painted in shades of gray to match the rock outcrops.

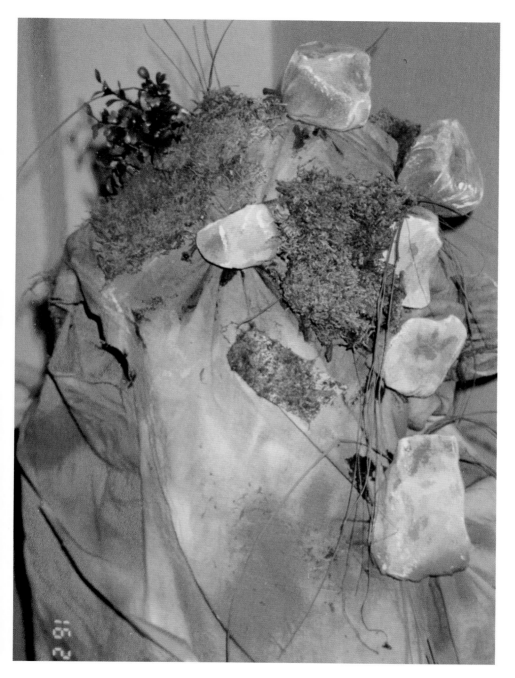

ABOVE: While looking bizarre at close range this sniper hood is actually very effective from distance. The sniper has attached very light polystyrene "rocks" to the hood in order to give it a 3D effect and to add depth to his outline.

ABOVE: A different approach to the high altitude camouflage problem. Here a student has cut the jacket full length in zigzag lines to provide depth and texture to his suit. The author found that normal spray paint worked just as well.

ABOVE: A tried and tested method of camouflaging has been re-thought to provide a camouflage option for the face. The design is that of the World War II German sniper's face veil and it is easy to make and very effective.

Carabiner. This essential item of climbing equipment can be found throughout most armies, although the practice among many soldiers of carrying a number of these shiny, stainless steel clips dangling from their belts is poor discipline and compromises camouflage.

The rifle. Like many military and police sniper units, the German Army selected the British-built Accuracy International AW rifle, under the designation *Scharfschützen-gewehr 22* (G22), as best able to suit the needs of their mountain warfare snipers. The German version has a folding stock and is chambered for the .300-caliber Winchester Magnum round, which has a much greater muzzle velocity than the basic model, resulting in a flatter trajectory as well as a longer and more consistent range, all of which are essential in the distance-dominated world of mountain warfare. The German Army also issues a tactical suppressor with each rifle; this aids concealment by limiting an enemy's ability to locate the firer by the sound of the weapon firing. Curiously, the Germans do not also issue subsonic ammunition, which would give their snipers a fully silenced option. The rifle also has a detachable bipod, weapon drag-bag, sling, laser rangefinder, and transit metal boxes, giving the German snipers a really excellent, all-round sniper system.

Rangefinders. Another vital piece of equipment for the mountain sniper is a rangefinder. The German optical industry, which has been one of the finest in the world for over a century-and-a-half, today produces the excellent Vectronix Vector laser rangefinder. This device includes a built-in compass that works in either degrees or mils, which enables the sniper to take the range, angle, and bearing all from the one piece of equipment.

Angle shooting

In lowland shooting it is unlikely that there will be a significant difference in heights between the sniper and his target. In mountains, however, there could well be considerable differences, which will affect the accuracy of the shot; as applies in almost every situation regardless of location or altitude, if the sniper misses with the first, he very rarely gets a chance for a second. To overcome this, German mountain snipers have developed a rapid and easy method for allowing the accurate engagement of targets both up- and downhill from the sniper. The data have been prepared based on the .300 WinMag round, which they use, but could easily be recalculated for use with other cartridges or for ranges in yards rather than meters. The method is based on the vertical angle between the firer and his target, and by working through an easy mathematical equation the correct range setting is reached for the individual sniper and this particular shot. For the method to be effective, the sniper must know the correct range setting (i.e., the number of clicks) for his rifle at each range from 100 to 1,000 meters, as this is the start point for the formula.

First, the sniper ranges the target, for which laser rangefinders are the quickest and most accurate method. Next, he assesses the angle between his firing position and the target, using a clinometer. With this infor-

RIGHT AND BELOW: The Austrian Army camp that sits at around 2,000 feet above sea level is a very well equipped training facility. Here two German mountain soldiers using the fitted shot marker facility check-zero their rifles prior to mountain work. This system allows the fall of shot to be seen, and hence adjusted, from the firing point, thereby obviating the need to keep visiting the targets and wasting time.

mation he refers to the issued chart (Table I) and locates the percentage drop associated with the angle.

Having established the percentage drop, the sniper then works out the drop relative to the range to this specific target, and arrives at a new range, and hence the new number of clicks to add to his sight. This new range takes into account the change in the weapon's ammunition ballistic curve due to the angle of the shot, and hence allows the sniper to achieve a highly accurate first round hit.

Table I: Percentage drops in range

Angle firer: target (degrees)	Range reduction (percent)	Range reduction (fraction)
10	1	1/100
15	5	1/20
20	7	1/14
25	10	1/10
30	15	1/6
35	20	1/5
40	25	1/4
45	33	1/3
55	50	1/2
65	65	2/3

ABOVE: A sniper observes his arc for enemy activity while his partner confers with another sniper team. The harsh terrain means it is unlikely that the snipers will be surprised by the enemy and so to a certain extent they can relax.

RIGHT: An experienced British Army sniper uses the issued ski poles to support his rifle while engaging targets high up in the surrounding mountains. This method has been used for years and provides a very stable shooting platform.

Table II: Sniper's range settings

Range (meters)	200	300	400	500	600	700	800	900	1,000
Clicks on sight	3	11	13	20	27	32	41	52	67

The way the system works can be clarified by means of an example:

- **Step 1.** The sniper acquires a new target that is at a higher altitude than him. He takes the range, using his laser rangefinder; it is 500 meters.
- **Step 2.** The sniper uses his clinometer to measure the angle from his position to that of the target; it is +20 degrees.
- **Step 3.** From Table I he reads off that an angle of 20 degrees gives a range reduction of 7 percent.
- **Step 4.** He calculates that 7 percent of 500 = 35 meters.
- **Step 5.** Thus, the adjusted range is 500 minus 35 meters = 465 meters.
- **Step 6.** He now calculates the new sight setting. From Table II he sees that the number of clicks on the sight between 400 and 500 meters is 7; therefore each click represents $100 \div 7 = 14$ meters. Hence 65 meters = $65 \div 14 = 5$ clicks. (Obviously, this calculation must be rounded-off to the nearest whole number.)
- **Step 7.** The sniper sets his sights at 400 meters = 13 clicks, then adds 65 meters = 5 clicks for a total of 18 clicks.

The keys to this method are the knowledge of the individual settings in number clicks for all ranges, and a method of measuring the angle between the firer and the target. With this information and the drops associated with each angle, the new

sight-setting can be quickly worked out, applied, and the shot taken.

Operations in mountainous regions

Mountainous operations are full of difficulties and require detailed planning if the sniper teams are to be employed effectively and survive. Various factors contribute towards a successful mission.

Climatic conditions. The weather becomes a very important aspect of day-to-day life for mountain troops and one that, if ignored, can have a far more dangerous effect than the enemy. A low temperature on its own does not always mean a life-threatening situation, but when combined with other common mountain elements it can quickly lead to injury and death. The speed with which the weather can change is alarming, and will kill the sniper, if ignored. For this reason the sniper teams must be prepared to react to every eventuality. This will inevitably result in heavy loads being carried, and reaffirms, yet again, the need for snipers to stay in peak physical condition.

Resources. The barren and rugged nature of the mountains means that resupply and the sustainability of the sniper team will be hazardous and difficult to achieve, not only because of the enemy, but also because of the remoteness and nature of the terrain. For

RIGHT: Mountain snipers begin the long haul up the mountains to take up OP and shooting positions. These snipers are moving in light order and would have to carry considerably heavier rucksacks if this were a longer deployment.

that reason the snipers will have to carry with them all the supplies needed for the duration of their task. This will obviously have an impact on the duration of their mission and, as a general rule, a period of forty-eight hours would be the normal limit before the team requires resupply, is relieved by a fresh team, or withdraws from the position. A possible alternative is that prior to taking up their position the team caches its resupply items in some convenient spot that can then be reached while still maintaining the arcs of responsibility.

Terrain and positioning. The sniper's ability to observe and locate an enemy at considerable distance in mountainous terrain means that even enemy reconnaissance troops or Special Forces, with their very high standards of camouflage and concealment, are likely to find it very hard to get past well-positioned sniper teams. Ground selection for the

ABOVE: A British sniper moves quickly across the exposed mountainside towards his intended OP location. Any kind of movement in the mountains is hard work; therefore snipers need to have above average fitness in this environment.

snipers is essential and some of the snipers should be sited in the most dominating positions, combined with others in areas that the enemy just would not think of looking at; this will lead the enemy into several intended killing areas, where their strength and morale will be hit from several different directions. The key areas for consideration are as follows:

- High ground on the flanks of the main access route.
- Approaches to high ground.
- High ground that will provide long range observation.
- Any possible flanking routes.

ABOVE: The effectiveness of the gray sniper suits is illustrated here: the instructor standing over the snipers draws the eye due to the color of his camouflage, while the snipers at his feet go almost unseen.

ABOVE: Here is a good indication of the effectiveness of the gray spray-paint, as the two snipers wearing brown camouflage are readily seen whereas the sniper in gray to their left is a much harder man to spot.

If possible the snipers should position themselves to make maximum use of the natural features of the surrounding area. This may include covering an approach route that has deep ravines or difficult open terrain either side, thereby confining the enemy to a selected and deadly killing area. With interlocking arcs of fire and additional area protection, using claymore and other types of mine, the snipers should be able to occupy positions that will render large areas untenable to the enemy. In this context, a ridgeline seems, at first sight, to be too obvious and exposed a position to be occupied by a sniper team, but with the right camouflage and careful selection of the actual location this will enable the snipers to achieve the maximum observation and fire arc, and will deny a larger area to the enemy. (It should be noted also that a ridgeline is also a difficult target for both artillery and mortars, since their operators are unable to judge the fall of shot and thus adjust their fire as well as they can on other types of ground.)

LEFT: A concealed sniper aims at his target moving high in the mountains above him. The use of rangefinders greatly speeds up the response time to targets of opportunity like this.

BELOW: German mountain troops prepare to engage targets across the valley. Note the extended ray shield fitted to the telescopic sight to prevent the possibility of the sun reflecting off the scope's objective lens and compromising their location.

Communications and support. Radio communications are notoriously difficult in mountainous terrain. This means that the sniper team may not have guaranteed links to its superior headquarters or supporting units. For this reason detailed thought and careful planning are required to ensure that unit cohesion is maintained and that sniper teams do not become isolated and unsupported.

Snow. An obvious and common element of operations in the mountains is that of snow.

Snow will vary depending on the prevailing conditions, with higher temperatures producing more compact snow and lower temperatures producing drier and less compact snow. Snow reduces snipers' ability to move, increases the workload, and becomes a drain on energy levels. Frozen snow, when flat, makes movement possible, but steep frozen snow is slippery and dangerous, and requires climbing equipment and ropes for safe traverses. Soft snow, on the other hand, is less hazardous, but crossing it is both time-consuming and energy-sapping, meaning that time, distance, and fitness levels have to be factored into any plan.

Wind chill. It is essential to maintain the body's core temperature in the mountains, but the presence of a wind will greatly increase the problem. The higher the wind the greater will be the loss of heat from someone who is not properly protected,

which can lead, first, to a rapid degradation of personal performance and, ultimately, to death. This condition is known as wind-chill and is one of the main contributors to death in harsh conditions.

Shelter

Sniper teams require either access to shelter or the knowledge of how to construct one, from whatever materials are available on the mountain. Extreme weather will quickly reduce a sniper team's effectiveness, so the ability to construct even the most basic shelter, even if only a wind-break, will enhance their fighting ability and operational duration. If a full (i.e., enclosed) shelter is

LEFT: A sniper pair stick close to a huge bolder and its associated shadow to adopt a shooting option. Note how the light reflects off the objective lens.

WIND SPEED (MPH)	LOCAL TEMPERATURE (°C)										
	0	-5	-10	-15	-20	-25	-30	-35	-40	-45	-50
	EQUIVALENT TEMPERATURE (°C)										
Calm	0	-5	-10	-15	-20	-25	-30	-35	-40	-45	-50
5	-5	-7	-12	-17	-23	-28	-33	-38	-44	-49	-55
10	-8	-14	-20	-26	-32	-38	-44	-50	-56	-62	-68
15	-11	-18	-25	-32	-38	-45	-52	-59	-66	-72	-79
20	-14	-21	-28	-35	-42	-49	-56	-63	-70	-77	-84
25	-16	-23	-31	-38	-45	-52	-60	-67	-74	-81	-89
30	-17	-25	-33	-40	-47	-55	-63	-70	-77	-85	-93
35	-18	-26	-34	-42	-50	-58	-66	-74	-82	-90	-98
40	-19	-27	-35	-43	-51	-59	-67	-75	-83	-91	-99
45	-19	-27	-35	-43	-51	-59	-67	-75	-84	-92	-100
45	-20	-28	-36	-44	-52	-60	-68	-76	-85	-93	-100
	Little danger		Considerable danger				Grave danger				

ABOVE: This windchill chart demonstrates clearly how icy winds can dramatically force down the ambient temperature as wind speed increases.

ABOVE: In the harsh mountain warfare environment snipers must be able to improvise and construct shelters for themselves. Here a simple lean-to shelter made from locally found timber will shield them from mot of the wind.

ABOVE: In deep snow the sniper pair may be forced to dig a snow hole both to protect them and conceal them. The roof can be made from ice, or a poncho and ski poles can be used with soft snow covering it to add camouflage.

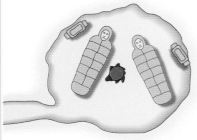

ABOVE: In snow conditions, snipers may have to dig their position out of the snow itself. Here a sniper pair in a circular hide conceal themselves in snow and overhanging branches.

constructed, it must have adequate ventilation, particularly if cookers are to be used inside, to avoid asphyxiation. Some of the following are options for the sniper teams:

Natural caves. Provide good overall shelter, but are not as prevalent as may be anticipated and, in any case, are unlikely to be in the position required.

Snow shelters. Snow can be fashioned into several different forms of shelter (e.g., igloo or snow-hole) and will provide snipers with adequate protection.

159

Tents. Tents provide snipers with protection but add to the load to be carried.

Natural materials. Natural materials, such as fallen trees, either on their own or in combination with snow, can be fashioned into wind-breaks.

Snow shelters. A snow-hole is easy to use and provides both warmth and natural camouflage for sniper teams. All that is needed for a two-man hole is a drift approximately nine feet wide and six feet deep. One man tunnels while the second excavates the spoil and maintains a sentry position for protection. Once a tunnel some six to eight feet long has been produced it can be expanded to produce the sleeping and living area,

whose exact style depends on snow depth, angle of drift, and the team's personal preferences. Once constructed, the entry point is closed by a moveable block of snow; care must be taken to ensure that an open ventilation hole is maintained throughout the team's stay, with the sentry usually monitoring this requirement.

An alternative to the snow-hole is the snow-trench, which is, in effect, a snow-hole that is excavated vertically rather than horizontally. This is dug in exactly the same way as the normal infantry trench and the floor is

BELOW: A sniper uses the cover of fir trees to conceal himself while lining up for shot on the mountainside. The use of the ski poles in this scenario greatly increases the sniper's ability to hit with the first round.

then covered with wood (for example, branches) and all equipment is placed inside prior to the roof being fitted. If the snow is well compacted, snow blocks can be cut and used to form the roof; if not, ski-poles can be laid across to support a waterproof fabric layer, which is then covered with loose snow, and this serves as both camouflage and insulation.

Natural foliage. A combination of snow and trees or branches can be used at lower altitudes to make a "tree bivvy" (bivouac). This requires a circular trench to be dug in

the snow under the tree canopy, with the tree's foliage being used as both camouflage and protection from the elements. In areas where the snow is not deep enough, the snipers can cut wood from trees and make two woven sides to use as wind-breaks. By leaning these against a suitable tree, the snipers can create a double-sided lean-to that will provide them with a level of protection and camouflage from the elements and enemy. A third lean-to will provide for a three-sided shelter and give additional protection from the elements.

Natural fuels. The sniper will always benefit from the knowledge of nature, and in such a cold and unforgiving area, knowledge of natural fuels could prove to be the difference

BELOW: A pair of German mountain snipers line up on targets high in the mountains. The mountain sniper course is evenly split between firing at higher and lower targets.

between life and death. Wood is a common and often-found base for fire and warmth. Dry and dead wood provide the best material for burning, but birch and willow will burn even when wet. Peat is a natural fire source, as is dry long grass, and even animal dung can be used as a fuel for fire and hence warmth.

Camouflage. Mountains require a completely different approach to camouflage compared to that used at lower altitudes, and much will depend upon the snipers' ability to improvise. One interesting and very effective method used by German mountain troops when operating in barren, rocky terrain is to spray random patches of gray paint on their issue white over-suit. Another aspect is that of sound, which travels considerable distances in the otherwise silent mountains, and great self-discipline must be exercised to avoid giving out any loud or unusual noise (for example, by allowing two metal objects to bang together) that might help the enemy to locate the team's position.

The differing levels and rock structures, coupled with the shades and shadows, create a good area within which a sniper can conceal himself. However, one problem he must guard against is that of vaporization, a natural phenomenon at high altitude, where warm air exhaled by humans or from a weapon being fired can freeze in the colder air, creating a cloud of fog that then hangs in the air. Such telltales are a sure indication to a watchful enemy that something potentially hostile is sheltering there.

On the lower slopes a tree line usually provides snipers with a natural area for hiding, and all their normal techniques will come into play in their tactics for concealment. Once above the tree line wintry weather will give an almost unbroken white condition in which to disappear, while summer conditions will be shadow and rock, or a mixture of snow and rock; both circumstances can be easily mastered by the sniper team to give an advancing or retreating enemy a serious problem to contend with. Any movement should be masked as well as possible, especially if it involves movement across snow.

Snipers crossing snow must utilize any available shadow or natural lines of breakage in the snow, such as changes in rock pattern, where disturbed snow will not look out of place. The age-old trick of using a fallen tree branch to brush away tracks works, to a certain extent, and is, of course, performed by the last man in the team. It serves to lessen the outline and confuse the instigator's identity, but will inevitably still leave some traces of disturbed snow and so cannot be assumed to be the perfect concealment option. Extreme care must be taken to avoid making any form of track leading directly to camouflaged positions, as this will be like an indicator beacon that the position is occupied and thus serve as a magnet for artillery rounds!

Visibility restrictions. In mountainous operations variations in weather conditions will restrict visibility at different times of the day and night. The following may be encountered and must be understood and accounted for in the overall plan:

- White-out: wind-driven loose snow reducing visibility to a few yards.

ABOVE: A British sniper in snow overwhites uses a snow veil to conceal his location against fresh snow. In this scenario the sniper must be careful not to create too much shadow and draw attention to his location.

• Cloud: operations at high altitude may take the sniper above the cloud base, again restricting visibility to a few feet.

Avalanches. Avalanches involve a large mass of snow, ice, and earth breaking away and descending downhill at great speed, sweeping aside or burying anything in its path. To avoid avalanches snipers should follow the following safety rules:

• Keep high and avoid triggering the avalanche yourself.
• Keep clear of snow build-up areas, particularly during and after storms.
• Avoid leeward slopes, as they are prone to slab slides.
• Never travel alone.
• Never expose more than one of the team to danger.
• Don't assume that because a colleague has passed over a dangerous area it is necessarily safe for you.
• The most dangerous slopes are between 30 and 45 degrees.
• Seek local advice.
• Check recent weather history.
• Snowfall greater than one inch per hour leads to avalanche danger.

Shooting positions

Mountainous terrain offers an abundance of fire positions, with its rocks and crags from which sniper teams can choose. If, however, they are required to adopt shooting positions on the move or immediately after breaking they will have to improvise and use whatever is around them to create a stable shooting position. On booted foot, the teams will make use of available terrain and foliage, but if on snow shoes or skis then knowledge and practice of accepted techniques will enable them to accurately engage an enemy.

Prone position. When adopting the prone position in snow, the sniper must ensure the weapon muzzle stays clear of the snow, otherwise an internal blockage might be created. Once down, the sniper can use snow shoes, rucksack or other equipment as a firing platform, and both he and his improvised firing platform should be pressed down

ABOVE: German mountain snipers in the Austrian Alps engaging high-altitude targets with their Accuracy International G22 rifles.

into the snow to provide the most stable positions as well as a certain level of protection from view and fire. If on skis, the sniper must spread his legs and ensure that the ski-tips are pointing outwards

Kneeling position. The kneeling position is similar to its use in other environments and the sniper's equipment will provide options for a stable shooting platform. If on skis the sniper must kneel with the rear leg angled towards the floor and the ski pointing out to the side at a 45-degree angle with the ski on its side. The ski-poles should then be held with the non-firing hand, with the ski-pole straps being used to provide a rest from which to shoot.

ABOVE: Shooting from skis is a tricky business. The positioning of the skis is the all important factor since it provides a stable base from which to shoot.

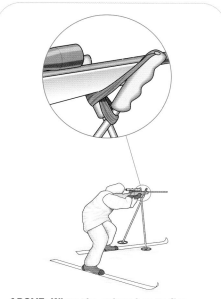

ABOVE: When the sniper has to fire while standing on skis, he can use the ski poles to help steady his aim.

BELOW: Shooting down into a valley with the Accuracy International G22 rifle. This and other methods taught during the German Army sniping-at-altitude course in Bavaria are very effective.

ABOVE: The mountain sniper must be an excellent all-round skier, sometimes using speed, sometimes endurance for the long haul to and from observations and firing positions. However, frequently stealthy movement while on skis is called for, and this requires much practice. Various methods are illustrated here.

Standing position. The standing position on skis is similar in principle to the kneeling position, with the supporting leg being angled out at about 45 degrees to aid balance, and the ski-poles being utilized to provide a stable platform from which to shoot.

Mountain patrolling and movement

Economy of effort is the basic overriding factor for all mountain troops. While professional mountaineers move slowly and deliberately, especially when climbing, such climbing is also done with short, measured steps following a zigzag track, allowing the snipers to carry heavy loads without over-exerting themselves. Also, wherever possible, the foot is placed flat and level, in order to reduce muscular stress and the chance of becoming unbalanced and then falling. When moving downhill the same zigzag is used, and overstepping or jumping down is avoided to prevent overstress of the knees and muscles. Scree and loose stones are to be avoided, since they can all too easily upset a sniper's balance and lead to injury or an uncontrollable fall.

The care required in moving, where every step has to be planned and executed with caution, may well lead to a decrease in the standard of observation. But, as in any other military movement, the snipers must remain alert and conscious of their surroundings, with frequent scans of the ground ahead and

RIGHT: The author engages targets in the valley below. A well-placed sniper would hold up a large force for some considerable time and could use a series of fallback positions to maximize disruption to the enemy.

around them to facilitate safe foot placement. Frequent halts will enable the snipers to scan the next section of their route as well as to rest, and they should be taken, wherever possible, in areas that offer good protection from view and fire. With a heavy load, a rate of advance of about two-and-a-half miles per hour should be feasible, with one additional hour for every thousand feet climbed or two thousand feet descended.

Navigation is much more difficult at altitude, although the arrival of GPS has greatly reduced the problems; nevertheless, the availability of this system cannot be assured, so the sniper must be able to rely on old-fashioned map-reading, if necessary. High altitude maps rarely have the same detail and accuracy as those of lower altitudes and in the absence of tracks and man-made features, such as roads, buildings, and churches, the sniper must rely on good compass skills and accurate pacing. With low cloud a constant problem, the ability to take bearings and altitude readings quickly is important, as these will enable the sniper to identify a specific feature and then use it as a back-bearing, to plot his position by reading the contours along the bearing. In dense cloud or fog, the angle of the slope and the altitude will provide the snipers with a start-point from which to carry out a map study and thereby locate the slope they are on by a process of elimination.

BELOW: A German Army mountain warfare instructor practices with his own rifle during a lull in training. Shooting is a perishable skill and so every chance to shoot should be taken.

General weather knowledge—northern hemisphere

- Weather systems move west to east.
- A red sunrise is bad and a red sunset is good.
- Sunset on a bright yellow sky indicates a windy day; pale yellow a rainy day.
- Heavy dew on cold clear nights indicates fog.
- Clearness of distant hills indicates a bad change in weather front.
- Weather changes for the worse usually come from the west or south- west.
- To find the area of low pressure put your back to the wind and the low will be on your left or rear left.
- Early morning rain rarely lasts: "rain before seven, gone by eleven."

Exposure

- Causes—cold, wind, moisture, fatigue, anxiety, illness, injury, wet clothing, lack of food, lack of water.
- Signs and symptoms—chill sensation, numbness, shivering, mild confusion, stumbling, feeling weak, falling, impaired functions, incoherence, irrationality, semi conscious, dilation of pupils, weak heartbeat and pulse, unconsciousness and death.
- Treatment—early recognition, shelter, warmth, heavily sugared foods and warm drinks, dry clothes, additional body heat from companion, cover extremities.

Cold weather injuries

- Exposure—due the body core temperature dropping below 35 degrees.
- Frost-nip—early symptoms of frost bite.
- Frost-bite—loss of circulating blood in extremities due to coldness.
- Trench foot—result of prolonged immersion in cold/wet conditions.
- Snow-blindness—result of reflection of the sun's ultraviolet rays off the snow.

Frostbite/frostnip

- Causes—cold, wind, moisture, restricted circulation.
- Signs and symptoms—cold and pain, skin color change with white patches, insensitivity to pain, stiffness of skin.
- Treatment—shelter; face, place hand over area; feet, place against warm skin; hands, place in armpits or in pockets.
- Do NOT—rub affected area, use direct heat.

Trench foot
- Causes—cold, moisture, lack of circulation.
- Signs and symptoms—persistent numbness, pain, throbbing, swelling.
- Treatment—remove boot, dry feet, rewarm with body contact, exercise.

Working at altitude and in cold weather conditions will have a direct effect on how an individual will perform even basic tasks, so training under such conditions is essential if a sniper team is to be employed. The human body is a highly balanced machine, and the temperature of its inner mechanisms is essential to its performance output. The body will convert any food eaten into fuel to provide both heat and energy levels for working, so a carefully structured diet is essential. The body will channel more of the food's fuel into body temperature the lower the temperature drops, and this reduces the energy output available for work, thereby reducing the amount of work achievable by the sniper. A sensible monitoring of clothing, shelter, and dietary intake will all go to reduce this effect and allow the sniper to work at a higher rate. However, below 32 degrees F a survival necessity will take over as the predominant factor; as a rule, the lower the temperature, the more it will affect the sniper's resolve and mental state.

LEFT: One look at the terrain beyond the sniper adopting the modified laid-back firing position illustrates the harshness and openness of the mountain region, and why snipers can so easily dominate it.

It is essential for the sniper teams to be properly equipped with clothing, food, and shelter, and that they are educated in the methods employed to reduce heat loss or overheating in order for them to be an effective fighting force. A layered system of clothing is best, with several layers of clothing being used to trap pockets of warm air in between so as to insulate the body when static. It is sensible to remove layers during periods of activity to ensure that the body does not produce sweat that will quickly chill against the body when activity ceases.

The food intake of a sniper in mountainous terrain is an area of great importance. With such a large percentage of the body's intake being diverted to provide body heat, a sniper must increase that intake to around six thousand calories a day, with calorie-rich items such as chocolate being high on the menu. The body will also require a greater intake of water under these conditions, so this must also be planned for in the sniper's preparations prior to deployment, be that training or operational. Dehydration will not be so obvious under cold conditions, so a commander must monitor his men's daily intake, which can vary due to work rate between about 1.75 and 10.5 pints a day. Liquid intake should be centered on hot, sweet drinks such as tea, coffee, and soup, and alcohol should never be consumed since it opens the pores of the skin and can lead to a quick loss of body temperature.

A daily working routine must be quickly established and maintained by all to eliminate unnecessary injury or degradation of a unit's effectiveness. Basic hygiene is the pivotal element in every operational theater, and mountain/cold weather scenarios are no exception. Daily washing of face, hands, crotch, and armpits will remove the chances of sore skin injuries. Shaving opens the skin pores, so it is best done last thing at night, behind shelter or inside a tent for protection from the elements. Hair growth or full beard will help protect from the elements, but if there might be a requirement to wear a respirator, then this may not be an option.

Wet clothing should be removed at the end of every day and replaced with dry to enable the wearer to have a comfortable sleep, while his wet clothing is dried using the heat of the sleeping bag. In the morning the wet clothing, even if it is not fully dry, must be put on again in order to maintain at least one set of dry clothing for wear at night. This may be easier said than done, but the commander must ensure his men carry out this unpleasant task. In any event, having donned the wet clothing, it soon warms up, because of the increase in body temperature due to increased work rate.

Effects on equipment

The low temperature conditions associated with high altitude work have an effect on operational equipment, so this is another area with which the sniper team must be fully conversant if they are to avoid a lowering of operational standards and performance.

Weapons. Normal lubricants often thicken and result in sluggish weapon action in low temperatures, so weapons should normally be cleaned and dried, and kept in this condition, with lubricant being applied

Cold weather mnemonic (British Army)

• Cold feet
C Keep clothing Clean, dirty clothing has less insulation properties.
O Avoid Overheating, sweat chills.
L Wear clothing Loose and in Layers, trapped air insulates.
D Keep clothing Dry, socks, underclothes and boots will dry in a sleeping bag.

F Fit your clothing properly.
E Exercise your fingers, toes, and face to keep circulating going.
E Eat well and drink well, no alcohol, food is energy.
T Tight boots are Terrible, they restrict blood flow and reduce movement.

only when needed. It is also important to note that, when a weapon is taken from the cold into a warmer shelter area, condensation will be formed and cleaning should not be attempted until this process has dried up. When moving or not in use, weapons should have muzzle, sight, and breech covers fitted to reduce the risk of snow and ice intrusion and damage. Finally, when a very cold weapon is fired, the temperature of the metal will rise rapidly, which can lead to breakage of some of the smaller parts of the weapon, such as firing-pins and extractors. Therefore, spares should always be carried. Another point to note is that if the weapon has been zeroed at higher temperatures, it will impact below its normal point in sub-zero temperatures.

Ammunition. It is important for all the factors of altitude, temperature, and air density to be considered and monitored by the team with regard to ammunition. Very cold weather will cause gunpowder to burn more slowly than normal, which may affect both recoil and trajectory, and the sniper team must be fully aware of the effects on the specific ammunition they intend to use.

Communications. Cabling and thin metal parts of radio and communications equipment are susceptible to damage under cold conditions, and condensation is a constant problem. Radios must not be taken out into the cold if condensation is present, and when brought in they should be wrapped in a dry covering such as a blanket. Batteries will be affected by cold and will give up to one-third less power than normal, so where possible they should be warmed before use, and never allowed to drop below two-thirds full charge.

Bullet penetration

Levels of protection from small arms fire will be achieved from the following preparations:
- New snow—thirteen feet.
- Wind driven snow—eight feet.
- Packed snow—seven feet.
- Ice—three feet.

Conclusion

The very nature of mountains means that many of the normal military practices and assets have to be modified, if they are to be of any use. For example, in mountainous areas roads for the movement of armor, artillery, and resupply vehicles are few, with the result that those that do exist are of great strategic and operational importance. To use snipers to delay an advancing enemy will have a major impact on his plans, while his ability to take out the sniper positions will be severely hampered by the restriction in vehicular movement off the road and the lack of good fire positions. This means that the enemy will have to deploy his infantry, since they are the best means available to close in on the snipers or to use accurate firepower to force them to move, but every such deployment will take time. The enemy infantry will be able to utilize the rocks and cover available in order to close with the snipers, and although this will present the snipers with a multitude of dismounted infantry targets, they cannot all be watched at once. But competent snipers will have a fall-back plan and, at a suitable point in the contact, they will withdraw and allow the enemy to overrun the first sniper position and then start to continue the advance, whereupon the snipers will engage them again and force them to deploy for a second attack, and so on. Such a delaying tactic can go on for as long as the snipers can get away with it, and if they have had the time to carry out reconnaissance and select multiple firing positions, this period could be considerable. It will also prove to be costly for the enemy, in manpower lost, time lost, and in force morale.

THE SNIPER IN DESERT AREAS

A very large proportion of the world's natural oil resources are located in countries with predominately desert environments. If these are to be protected, it is obvious that the majority of armies, and especially those likely to get involved in international operations, should plan for deployments in such terrain. Indeed, the pattern of events over the past thirty years shows that it is highly probable that the Middle East will be the scene of further conflict and that the world's oil supply will always be a factor in such events.

Desert conditions

Much of the desert landscape is of the barren, open type with large, unobstructed vistas where long-range observation is possible, an environment particularly suited to the sniper's skills. Even in the hilly and rocky areas of a desert the sniper can operate with

BELOW: The desert is not all sand, as most people believe, and is covered by broken rock in many areas. Here snipers train in the Kuwaiti desert prior to the 1991 Gulf War.

great effectiveness. Recent conflicts in such areas have seen an increase in the use and deployment of sniper teams, as commanders have come to realize that they are one of his most valuable tactical assets.

Deserts can have most unforgiving climates and any attempt to deploy and operate under these conditions without adequate planning and training will inevitably result in disaster. But, with good preparatory training and a professional attitude towards day-to-day life, the desert can become not just tolerable but even a very acceptable place in which to fight. Several factors need to be addressed before any unit deploys into a desert environment.

Terrain variations

The popular image of deserts, as enthusiasti-

cally promoted in Hollywood movies, is of rolling sand dunes where vehicles sink up to their axles, but the truth is very different. Of course, there certainly are areas of dunes and others of loose sand, but there are also a wide variety of other types of terrain, and a sniper unit must be aware of all these in order to plan and train realistically, and to pack the equipment they are likely to need.

Sand areas. Sandy areas can provide both good and bad conditions for movement, whether on foot or in a vehicle. A thin layer of sand will allow fast vehicle movement, although tracks can become a hazard after

BELOW: The vast openness of the desert lends itself perfectly to sniping. Such conditions are ideal for long-range weapons such as the .338- and the .50-caliber rifles.

ABOVE: The desert can be very hard going in places, with large hills and outcrops rising above vast, flat surrounding areas, which can be dominated by well-placed snipers.

BELOW: It is almost impossible to maneuver in wadis and jehels. Wadis can be great for moving in dead ground but bring with them the threat of ambush or even flash flooding from surrounding hills.

ABOVE: The desert can also be surprisingly green in places, and many a sniper has wished he had brought his rural ghillie suit with him on the deployment.

rain, because they set like concrete and can be very dangerous if hit at speed. But, the deeper the sand, the more difficult it is to maintain any speed, or sometimes to make any progress at all, without constant enforced halts to dig out one or more vehicles. Rolling sand dunes in general have steady gradients on the windward side and sharp inclines on the leeward side, making driving and movement difficult, but they can be traversed by vehicles fitted with wide wheels and appropriate tires.

Rock. As a result of thousands of years of harsh weather, the rocks in the desert are often sharp and deeply pitted, which can have a disastrous effect on all but specially designed vehicle tires. For the snipers, who may have to set up and occupy an OP in such rocky terrain, digging-in is simply not an option. The best solution is to erect a protective wall of rocks, a device known by its local Arab name of a *sangar*. Often the most practicable way of doing so is by building such a wall as an extension of an existing rocky outcrop, which reduces the work and also helps to camouflage the position by blending in.

Gravel. Large areas of most deserts are covered by large stones and rocks in a gravel base. At ground level, dead ground will often provide cover from direct observation. But, while some digging will usually be possible, this is very likely to be obvious from the air.

177

In general, concealment in this type of terrain is notoriously difficult.

Wadis. These are dry river beds and normally two contrasting types are found. The first of these are wide, shallow, sand-covered depressions, while the others are deep, rocky ravines. Both present obstacles to military movement. The shallow wadis are usually passable, although the soft sand can make for difficult going, especially for vehicles. On the other hand, the deep ravine wadi can provide a useful covert insertion route, albeit with limited options for cover from aerial observation. These deep wadis do, however, pose

ABOVE: This type of terrain was made for long-rang observation and shooting and as such is well suited to the sniper's skills.

RIGHT: British Army snipers occupy a roof space in their forward base in southern Iraq, providing long-range observation and fire when needed to protect their fellow soldiers.

two different types danger. The first, somewhat unexpectedly in view of the generally arid conditions, is the possibility of a flash flood that will, with little or no warning, sweep down the wadi, literally washing away anything in its path. The second problem with rocky wadis is that they make excellent sites for ambushes, giving those being ambushed nowhere to run.

Hills and escarpments. Desert regions are often broken up by large and long mountain or rocky outcrops that form significant obstacles to military movement. In such terrain, passes or other gaps assume great strategic and tactical importance, such as the Mitla Gap in the Sinai Desert. Snipers can be deployed to great effect in such terrain, either in defense to block an enemy advance, or, in an advance by locating and harassing defending enemy forces.

ABOVE: A sniper all but disappears in the rocky outcrop in the desert. From this advantageous position the sniper could seriously delay an advancing force, engage reconnaissance troops or just harass a defensive location.

Salt marshes. These are usually transitional areas between land and sea, and are normally found along the shore of estuaries and sounds, the salt content (salinity) being strong near the ocean but reducing to near fresh in up-river marshes. However, they can also be found far inland as well, particularly in desert regions, one of the most notorious being the *Dasht-e-Kavir* (= great salt desert) in north central Iran. (*Kavir* is the local word for a marsh.) This extends over an area some five hundred miles long by two hundred miles wide to the south-east of the Elburz mountains, where, since the climate is virtually rain-free with high surface evaporation, a salty crust has formed over a deep layer of marsh/mud. The result has the same characteristics and intense dangers as quicksand, making any form of military movement extremely hazardous.

Light

Fighter pilots and Hollywood producers both, quite rightly, make great play on the advantages of "attacking out of the sun," and this also holds good for sniper operations in the desert. In the early morning desert visibility is excellent, but as the ground heats up a haze forms that starts to shimmer, and eventually by afternoon mirages can be formed, severely affecting normal observa-

tion for the sniper. The effect is to make objects appear to separate, move, and rejoin, thereby making identification very difficult at ranges in excess of a thousand yards. Thermal image sights are the best observation aids in such circumstances, since they can still produce a heat image, but without them snipers must seek high ground to enable them to look down and overcome the worst effects of any shimmer or mirage.

BELOW: Snipers of The 1st Battalion, the Princess of Wales's Royal Regiment, manned their perimeter positions for almost a month during a recent operational tour of Iraq to repel constant attempts by insurgents to overrun the base.

From the top of a destroyed hardened aircraft shelter "somewhere in Iraq" U.S. Special Forces employ their sniper rifles to engage targets during Operation Iraqi Freedom.

Judging distance is also much more difficult under desert conditions, making range-finders of considerable value, although reflected light from their glass lenses can travel great distances, even piercing the haze, and thus betray an otherwise concealed position. Night operations can also be affected due to the reflective nature of the desert and the fact that a full moon will almost turn night into day. Conversely, when there is either no or only partial moonlight the desert is almost pitch black, making movement very slow and time-consuming. Today, the Global Positioning System (GPS) makes accurate navigation much more possible under such conditions, but the lack of ambient light still makes for slow and difficult movement for both vehicles and troops on foot.

Rain and snow

Rain and even snow in desert conditions are more common than realized, and this caused the death of at least one member of the ill-fated Bravo Two Zero patrol of the British SAS during the first Gulf War. When it does occur, rain can be very heavy and is not infrequently accompanied by lightning, which can be very dangerous—even life-threatening—for troops caught out in the open. Also, as mentioned above, any troops in a wadi should, if they receive any forecast or indications of rain, move out into more open terrain at once in order to avoid the flash floods that may well sweep down the valley.

Vegetation

Vegetation can be a good indicator of water, an ever-present concern under desert condi-

tions. Among the indicators of sub-surface water are: palm trees—water is three feet or less from the surface; salt grass—water is about six feet below; and willows—water is some twelve feet below. Such information can, quite literally, be the difference between life and death for a sniper unit on the move and without direct logistical support.

Acclimatization

Most soldiers of Western origin have no real concept of just how hot desert regions can be, the level of heat that greets them almost invariably coming as a total shock; indeed, in some extreme cases it has even resulted in premature death. Thus, it is essential that, wherever feasible, troops should be allowed a period of time to acclimatize themselves to the new surroundings. Such acclimatization should allow for initial periods of inactivity interspersed with ever-increasing levels of work and exercise, as their bodies adjust their cooling systems to accept the increased levels of physiological stress that the desert creates. If this is done correctly, lethargy will be slowly replaced by a return to normal levels of output and work, as the troops become accustomed to the new levels of energy they burn while working. To ignore this aspect of desert deployment is to subject troops to temperature-induced injuries such as heat-exhaustion and heat-stroke.

Cold temperatures

Because of the extremes of temperature that occur between day and night, desert conditions can just as easily kill a man through hypothermia as through heat-stroke. It is by no means unheard of to encounter snow in desert regions, and freezing rain is more common than is generally appreciated. The myth that the desert is always hot has claimed the lives of many men, and the tendency for a soldier to throw away warm clothing as he struggles in the heat of the day can all too often lead to death from the effects of the cold at night.

Water

The human body cannot be trained to function without water, and such an aim should never be attempted. As a general rule, in desert conditions the human body will require twice or three times the water intake compared to that in a temperate zone, and this must be a vital factor in any planning meeting. In the desert, even a person at rest will lose liquid through perspiration—the actual amount depends upon body size, but may be up to one pint per hour—and he or she must drink enough to replace this in the same period. When the soldier concerned is patrolling or working then the water requirement increases accordingly. A lesser intake may be feasible for a shorter period, but if the work-rate continues the water intake must be increased in direct proportion to the fluid lost during daily activity. The availability of water in the desert is so limited that a unit should always deploy with all the water it calculates it will need. It is certainly true that a number of oases do exist, but they are much rarer in the Arabian peninsula than, say, in the Sahara, and these should be viewed only as an "extra" in the event that they are available at all.

Snipers must be fully aware and practiced

Signs of dehydration in increasing order of severity
- Thirst.
- Reduced activity.
- Marked loss of appetite.
- Nausea.
- Tiredness.
- High body temperature.
- Headache.
- Dizzy spells.
- Loss of sensation in the limbs.
- Breathing difficulty.
- Speech becomes slurred and reactions become slower.
- Unconsciousness.

in all methods of obtaining water under desert conditions. They should always carry enough water for their task, but the knowledge of how to improvise will allow some hope of survival in the worst of scenarios. The solar still works by condensation, and is created by digging a small hole in an area of increased moisture, as indicated by plant life or damp sand, and placing a plastic covering over the hole, held in place by stones or other suitably heavy objects. The sun then extracts the moisture from the ground in the form of condensation, which forms on the plastic sheeting and can be collected in a suitable container placed in the base of the hole.

The expression "water discipline" is often interpreted as meaning going without water for extended periods, even when it is available, but this is not correct. Water should be drunk frequently when it is

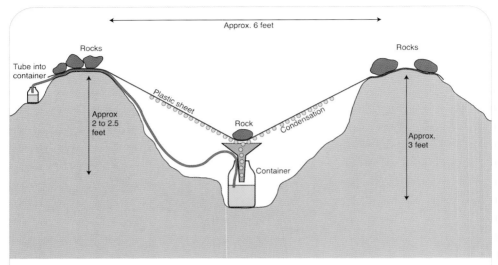

ABOVE: A solar still that could provide vital drinking water for the sniper, who will be expected to work alone for long periods.

available, as not to do so will weaken the soldier and decrease his work output. Water discipline is about drinking when told to do so, drinking from authorized places only, and not complaining when water is scarce—it does not mean that the soldier must deprive himself of available water.

One technique is to drink excessive quantities of water prior to deployment, since it is possible to build up a store in the body. This will not only allow for sweating but will also enable the person concerned to carry out normal work rates. This effect can be achieved by slowly increasing the quantities of water drunk, thereby reducing the tendency to be sick, until the person can drink an amount of water that is considerably above his or her actual daily intake needs. This will provide the body with what is, in effect, a second water-bottle upon which it can draw by natural processes.

Heat injuries

The risks associated with over-exposure to the sun's ultra-violet rays for extended periods of time are very real, and soldiers must be educated as to how quickly the sun can cause not only injury but even death in extreme cases. Most soldiers from temperate countries equate a suntan with a supposedly glamorous image, so that when they are placed in an environment where they can acquire one with little effort they fail to understand the dangers. But, in reality, it is essential that they remain covered from the sun's rays and use protective creams where available, as well as ensure an adequate water intake.

Heat injuries can be avoided by working at a lesser rate where feasible, resting frequently, and by wearing the appropriate protective clothing. Sunglasses reduce the risk of eye fatigue, although care must be taken to

ensure that they do not compromise camouflage and concealment and draw the attention of an enemy sniper! It is also advisable to avoid lying down in the heat, as the air at ground level can be several degrees hotter than at a couple of feet above ground, so sitting up while resting is actually more beneficial. Alternatively, if the soldier is likely to be in the same location for an extended period of time, getting below ground level will be cooler since it can be up to fifteen degrees cooler approximately eighteen inches below ground level.

Heat cramps and exhaustion

The loss of salt from the body's system can lead to painful muscle cramps that usually involve the abdominal area and the extremities. This can be remedied by the controlled intake of a saline solution to replace the lost salt from the system, preferably under medical or paramedical supervision.

ABOVE: A sniper of the Royal Irish Regiment occupies a perimeter position during the liberation of Iraq. The black humor so often associated with British soldiers is well illustrated with his improvised sign.

Heat-stroke

Heat-stroke is the result of the body's cooling system breaking down—absence of sweating is one indication of its onset—and it can lead to death. It can be induced by heavy work rate, diarrhea or failure to acclimatize properly. The symptoms of heat-stroke can mirror those of heat-exhaustion, with the lack of sweating and redness to the skin being other key signs. The onset of this condition can occur with extreme suddenness and so the early symptoms must be identified and treated quickly if serious illness or death is to be avoided.

Other factors

Local history. It is essential that any unit deploying into another nation's country

ABOVE AND BELOW: The desert is a wonderful mix of the harsh and the surreal: there's nothing for miles one minute, and the next a human (friend or foe?) appears as if from nowhere. The expanse of dead ground and the ability to be concealed quickly can make this terrain deadly to the unwary.

should take the time to learn and understand its people, their lifestyle, and their religion. This is of particular importance in a desert environment where the indigenous inhabitants almost always have a very simple and uncomplicated approach to life, with the majority living just above the bare subsistence line. Thus, a Western army with its abundance of weaponry and materiel, and—of striking importance in the desert, where such things are in very short supply—vast quantities of food and water, can easily appear overwhelming and cause antagonism, simply by being there.

Clothing and equipment

The desert will demand a variation, or at least a change, in the method of wearing clothing and of carrying equipment when compared to European or other temperate theaters. The desert will pose an extreme of hot and cold that will have to be considered, since, as described above, either will seriously injure or kill a sniper who has not made the proper preparations. Everyday uniform has to be both hardwearing and cool to wear during the day in order to avoid overheating and the resulting degradation in the sniper's performance, but it also has to be warm and capable of forming part of a layered defense against the cold at night.

Footwear is another important area and one that seems to create problems in many armies, primarily because so many procurement agencies seem to think that they can economize with impunity.

Not only is the heat to be considered, but also the going; sand is a particular problem for both boot and wearer, while rock and gravel are extremely destructive on both the soles and the uppers of the boots. Thus, normal high leg boots, which may be ideal in temperate climates, are both uncomfortable and too hot for everyday use in desert conditions, and so a suitable lower-leg durable boot must be found. Manufacturers have now produced a plethora of designs to meet this need, but sadly in many armies the soldiers are forced to buy them on the civilian market as they are not available through the quartermaster's stores.

For the sniper, a suitably colored and sturdy boot must be identified. Sniper teams will usually put the boot through more rigorous testing than the average infantryman, who will not be dragging his boots across rocky ground or camouflaging them with everything from vegetation to paint.

Camouflage and concealment

No matter where he deploys or in what the terrain, of paramount importance to the sniper is being able to remain unseen by the enemy. Thus, to be aware of camouflage techniques for desert conditions is of equal, possibly even greater, importance than camouflage in rural settings in Europe or North America. In the wide expanse of the desert, whether the surface is rocky ground, gravel or sand, it is very difficult to camouflage and conceal men and equipment. Passive detection devices work over great ranges and any lapses in concealment discipline will almost inevitably result in the early detection of a position. Thus, the selection of the right colors and materials for uniforms, for example, is vital, and snipers should never think that one color will work in all desert

terrains or light conditions.

A selection of basic colors must be available to the snipers. Some manufacturers appear to be under the impression that the desert is a very light sand color and have produced equipment that is almost white in appearance, which is in reality, almost unusable on its own. A more common color to use as a base camouflage is *coyote tan* (technically known as H-235). Variations of this brown and the light sand, coupled with camouflage nets and basic skills, will assist the sniper in concealing himself.

Snipers must be able to adapt to any environment and must spend time studying the terrain and then find ways of emulating what he sees. This will normally consist of a combination of issued and improvised equipment, and, as for any other scenario, the sniper must be willing and capable of

ABOVE: A selection of different desert camouflage outfits, each with its own good and bad points: left to right, French, German, British, and American. A recently issued Jordanian digital pattern is one of the more effective.

forward thinking in order to disappear into his surroundings with minimal assistance.

Desert tactics

In the desert, as in any other combat arena, the aim is to destroy your enemy's will and his ability to fight and conduct operations, and the sniper is a very high value player in such warfare.

Reconnaissance. Identification of the enemy and early warning of his movements are essential, and the sniper's ability to conceal himself and to accurately observe over long range are vital assets to any commander.

ABOVE: A sniper pair observe over the open desert during operational deployment training in Kuwait. Apart from the intense heat, the rocky surface makes it far from comfortable to move across.

Positive identification will ensure that fratricide incidents remain at a minimum and that all relevant firepower can be focused on the enemy once he is identified. Sniper and other reconnaissance assets will be focused on the following:

- Locate and provide intelligence on the enemy.
- Locate indirect fire targets and control artillery and mortar assets.
- Obtain terrain information.
- Provide security screens against surprise attack.
- Raid operations.
- Deception plans.

The abundance of satellites and aerial platform intelligence means that ground reconnaissance can now be more specific in its nature, with recon troops and snipers being tasked with gaining intelligence on routes around an enemy, probing gaps in enemy defenses, determining terrain, and checking the extent of the enemy's radar and weapons coverage.

Long-range reconnaissance and raids. Snipers are well-suited to carry out long-range reconnaissance and raids against the enemy rear areas and support infrastructure. They can also be used to collect information on the enemy or to cause disruption to enemy defensive preparations or to an enemy forming-up for attack. Snipers can wreak havoc among any force, causing a disruption to normal daily routines, a drop in morale, and a rededication of resources and men to

remove the sniper threat. All of these combine to buy the snipers' commanders that all too rare commodity—extra time.

With an ever present lack of trained Special Forces and dedicated reconnaissance troops, snipers' skills can be used to assist in the following long-range tasks:

- Covert reconnaissance of enemy positions.
- Location of command positions.
- Location of major assets such as aircraft, armor, artillery, and radar.
- Direct artillery or aircraft attack.
- Removal of anti-air assets to clear a route for aircraft.
- Watch and report on enemy movements.
- Kill key enemy commanders and personnel.
- Provide distraction and deception actions.

Firepower. Indirect fire control and forward observer duties greatly enhance the sniper's ability to engage and destroy the enemy. The

ABOVE: Far from their green and pleasant homeland, the sniper platoon of the Royal Irish Regiment move in their WMIK Land Rovers through the Iraq desert on route to Al Amarah, north of Basra, during the Iraqi war.

sniper's ability to identify and engage key enemy equipment and personnel, and to provide maximum disruption, together with morale issues, are becoming ever more obvious to commanders in many armies, resulting in an increase in the numbers of snipers trained and deployed.

Surprise. Covert entry into an enemy's area or concealed stay-behind and ambush positions allows the snipers to engage the enemy at a time and point of maximum surprise.

Initiative and speed. Good knowledge of the area and conditions will allow the commander to gauge the speed and activity

ABOVE: Soldiers of the Royal Irish Regiment were the first British troops to arrive in Al Amarah during the Iraqi war. This town was to be the center of harsh fighting for the snipers of 1 PWRR.

levels he can maintain against the enemy, and so can deploy and engage at a faster rate than his opponent, thereby controlling the battle. Good pre-deployment planning will allow the snipers to be placed in or moved to areas best suited to their skills and movement abilities.

Multiple operations. The commander who can attack in several areas simultaneously, thus taking the fight to the enemy while not allowing him time to recover, will win the day. Snipers are a perfect tool to maintain the pressure on an enemy force once a larger attacking force has withdrawn. The snipers will set about never giving the enemy a

moment's peace or regroup time, and this will therefore affect the enemy's morale and will to fight.

Over-ground mobility. With the wide expanses often found in desert operations it is vital that snipers plan their mobility with great detail. A careful assessment of the enemy's capabilities will enable the snipers to make detailed plans of how mobile they need to be and what assets they need to bid for, such as vehicle drop-off, helicopter insertion or self-drive, since foot insertions are unlikely due to the vast distances that may have to be covered and the speed of this type of warfare. One option that is often used is the issue of all-terrain vehicles (ATVs) or quad bikes that allow fast deployment and are relatively easy to conceal when the snipers need to move forward into position on foot. These vehicles may be deployed with a medium-sized

193

ABOVE: A sniper of the Royal Irish Regiment relaxes between operations during the Iraq war. Note the Accuracy International .338-caliber sniper rifle located within easy reach on the wing of the Land Rover.

mother vehicle, such as a Land Rover, which will act as a re-supply vehicle for fuel and rations to allow protracted operations behind enemy lines.

To further enhance their deployment ability snipers should be trained for and have available the following insertion/extraction options:

- Parachute.
- Helicopter.
- Submarine/landing craft.
- Suitable overland vehicles.

Any movement in desert conditions has to be accompanied by suitable all-round

ABOVE: USMC helicopters were used extensively to deploy troops during the war, and several sniper teams were air-lifted into location to support offensive operations.

ister themselves as well, and that time must be allowed for this to happen.

Deception and covering force. Deception can play a very big part in open warfare, and snipers can be effectively used to draw an enemy into a selected killing area or to deflect an enemy away from a recovering unit. The preparation of a dummy defensive position and the occupation of it by snipers who have a planned fall-back route can be an effective deception measure if planned, prepared, and controlled correctly. Snipers can provide long-range firepower, thereby giving the impression of a much larger number of soldiers, going some way to confusing and deceiving the enemy.

The ability of snipers to locate and engage enemy reconnaissance forces, and compel them to deploy into fighting formation while restricting their observation can lead to an enemy being forced into

defense. Snipers mounted on suitable vehicles, such as ATVs, can be utilized as flank protection while the reconnaissance troops provide the forward screen. This protective option can also be used for a resting or static formation, thereby allowing the main force to recover or administer itself while the snipers provide early warning and delaying action. But it must be remembered that the snipers will need to rest and admin-

advancing blind. Alternatively, the enemy commander may assume that he has found the main force and deploy into battle formation, which will cause delay and use up vital enemy supplies, with the sniper force slipping away before they get too involved in a fight they are not strong enough to win. The snipers will require some form of firepower assistance to break cleanly from an enemy and this can be artillery, multi-launch rocket systems (MLRS), mortars or ground-support aircraft.

To maximize the disruptive effect on the enemy the snipers should fall back or move to flanking positions and utilize heavier calibers such as .338 and .50-caliber rifles to continue pressure on the enemy and deny him room or time to regroup or re-deploy; alternatively, a second line of snipers should

ABOVE: Snipers of 1 PWRR engage insurgents who have just ambushed the Warrior armored vehicles on patrol in southern Iraq. The battalion snipers returned home as the most experienced snipers in the British Army.

be ready to continue the fight after the withdraw of the initial force.

At some stage in the battle the enemy will lose momentum through casualties, confusion, and re-supply needs, and the snipers must be watching for this moment and then unleash a full-scale attack against key personnel and equipment already identified by them during the battle so far.

The enemy

The main area of focus for the snipers must be the level of training and skill the enemy possesses, coupled to the drive and desire to win, which can be national or religious in basis. Together this will spur an enemy on in moments of hardship and danger. To ignore this focus can lead to the snipers being placed at lethal risk. The snipers must deploy knowing that not only will the enemy be expecting them to be there somewhere, but that he has spent time preparing how he is going to kill them quickly and with as much violence as possible. As way of proof, the Iraqi insurgents produced a code of operations that they disseminated via the Internet and Arab TV stations in early 2005 for their own snipers to follow, and this included the following (translated):

• Target commanders and pilots, so as to attack the head of the enemy snake and handicap its command.
• Target enemy snipers and reconnaissance teams.

• Assist RPG teams and other *mujahideen* infantry.
• Shoot specialist targets like communications officers, tank crews, engineers, doctors, and chaplains for psychological reasons, and tank drivers while tanks cross obstacles so they crash and kill the whole crew.
• In urban fighting attack enemy instruments and fire from high positions to assist infantry assaults by controlling mortar and rocket fire.
• Target U.S. Special Forces; they are very stupid because they have a Rambo complex, thinking that they are the best in the world; don't be arrogant like them.

BELOW: A sniper's eye view of a vehicle patrol deep in a wadi. From his location he would be able to devastate this unit who have only limited cover and movement options.

CHAPTER 6 COUNTER-SNIPING

Counter-sniping is much more than the methodology of a sniper setting out to remove another sniper in some dramatic form of one-on-one duel. It is better described as a process by which one man with modern multi-media facilities at his disposal out-thinks another in order to prevent a threat from developing in the first place. The reason most units fail to develop a really effective counter-sniper capability is because they concentrate on the sniper-versus-sniper scenario, following the principle of "the only way to remove one sniper is with another one." In reality, the one-on-one situation should be the final option; it is far more important and effective to prevent the sniper setting up for business in the first place.

Why sniping is a threat
- Fast, accurate, and fear-inducing.
- Easy, inexpensive, and requires minimal trained manpower.
- Very difficult to defend against.
- Already been used and proven.
- It is only time before there is a terrorist sniper attack.

Units should employ experienced snipers to run their counter-sniper cells. They should be men or women who are capable of thinking "outside-the-box," and who will bring imagination and subtlety to enable them to negate the threat. All this knowledge and training is, however, of little value if the counter-sniper cell does not have access to good-quality and detailed intelligence, since, without reports of the enemy's activities and attacks, the cell leader cannot identify the enemy's method of operation.

Many countries claim to have counter-sniper teams and advisers, but the truth is that the majority of such people have little idea of what they are supposed to do nor how they should train for their mission. If the FBI (or any other U.S. agency, for that matter) had had a dedicated team of sniper-experienced intelligence analysts who were fed all information on rifle crime, the Washington Beltway Snipers, who wrought such havoc in 2002, might well have been identified much sooner. Nothing, of course, is certain and it might well be that even with such a team the killers might not have been identified, but at least the chances of doing so would have been greater. But this is not just a U.S. problem; many other countries also lack a dedicated staff to spend their time studying, planning, and training not only to defeat snipers once they have taken action, but also to initiate measures that might discourage them from acting in the first place.

ABOVE: Finnish troops carry out counter-sniper training under British supervision during cross training as part of a joint operation in the Balkans. Counter-sniping is a manpower- and time-intensive operation.

It is important, in this context, to appreciate that sniping is a range-independent tactic and not, as so many people seem to think, solely a long-range discipline. Of course, snipers do have the ability to shoot out to very long ranges with great accuracy, but they also have the ability to move unseen across any piece of real estate in full view of an enemy and remain unseen or take up a fire position, even at comparatively short range. Snipers also have a second weapon, that of inducing fear and paralysis over a wide area, when enemy individuals perceive that they are being shot at but have no idea where the shot is coming from. Such people, also, are not concerned whether the shooter is close by or far away, only that he is firing at them. Thus, distance shooting is but one aspect of the sniper's role.

The terrorist threat

A whole new range of frightening scenarios has opened up since the horrific use of civilian airliners in the "9/11" attacks on civilian and military targets within the continental USA. The world had long been used to such groups as the PIRA (Provisional Irish Republican Army), Hezbollah, Fatah, and Abu Nidal as they carried out attacks that occasionally received worldwide media coverage, but now another, international, fear-inducing name became more widely voiced—Al-Qaeda.

Likely civilian/industrial targets

- Petro-chemical facilities.
- Energy production facilities.
- Road/rail networks, particularly choke points.
- Airports/shipping/harbors.
- Emergency services.
- Factories and staff.
- Corporate business, particularly in the financial sphere.
- Food and water supplies/production.
- Communications hubs.

ABOVE: Damage to the Pentagon from the "9/11" attacks that brought home to the United States the severity of terrorism on a global scale. It can only be a matter of time before a sniper attack takes place.

This growing force in global terrorism is more accurately described as a "brand name," in which like-minded terrorists work in a loose confederation under the same symbolic banner. It is not, as some newspaper and TV pundits seem to believe, a tightly organized international force, directly controlled by a single command structure. That is not to say that Al-Qaeda's acknowledged leader Osama Bin Laden cannot reach far and wide, or that his personal influence does not have a grave consequence for those he targets, but rather that his personal control is sometimes over-played.

Combined with this, it has gradually come to be understood that a terrorist is not necessarily either a stupid or an ill-educated person. Some of the foot-soldiers may, indeed, be both, but many terrorists and the majority of their leaders come from well-educated, middle-class families, and virtually all have a genuine belief that what they are

ABOVE: Terrorist snipers would look to maximize the media attention in any attack they plan: if they could hit a fuel truck on an interstate highway it would cause local chaos and general trepidation, especially if several such targets were hit simultaneously. That would be big time news worldwide.

ABOVE: The premise of attacking innocent people during everyday tasks has already been horrifically illustrated by the Washington "Beltway" snipers. Attacks on such places as gas stations would not only bring fear to the population, but would also affect the economy.

doing is sanctioned by their particular faith. It is essential that these factors are considered when developing strategies and tactics necessary to defeat them.

Terrorists, like insurgents of the 1960s-1990s, are in no position to take on their adversary on military terms, nor are they prepared for the time-consuming and somewhat uncertain outcome of a political campaign. So they resort to terrorist methods, based on hit-and-run principles—essentially psychological warfare aimed at terrorizing the general populace of a target nation, or a country where a target nation has bases, or involvement or influence. The aim is to force the public into bringing such

BELOW: Military aircraft of all shapes and sizes are vulnerable to attack from accurate small arms fire, even the mighty Hind attack helicopter.

pressure to bear on their government that it will change its policies, although often the terrorist aim is to bring down the entire governmental structure as well. Such public fear is usually created in several ways:

• Carefully orchestrated use of violence and the threat of violence.
• Attacks on targets that are either difficult or impossible to defend.
• Symbolic, spectacular, and attention-grabbing acts, intended to gain publicity and engender fear.
• Creation of an image of invincibility.

Osama Bin Laden has long been linked to Islamic extremism. He has been very well trained (by the CIA, incidentally), and he also has a detailed knowledge of both U.S. and U.K. security practices. His brand of "spectacular" against the West—in particular, against the U.S., U.K., and Spain—has made terrorism into a global war. But, lacking the means to mount a military attack on such countries, he recruits volunteers from all manner of nations, not excluding the United States and the United Kingdom, to carry out, first, reconnaissance and, subsequently, actual attacks against what he considers to be suitable

BELOW: British soldiers face up to firebombs thrown from a hostile crowd. It is not uncommon for terrorist snipers to use such unrest to cover their attempts to kill soldiers who are focused on the crowd and forced into the open.

infrastructure targets across the globe.

Western nations anticipate increasing attacks against their economic infrastructure, in particular—and sniping is one of the easiest and most cost-effective means of carrying these out. Just as the United States was demonstrably unable to prevent the use of airliners against key targets, and Spain and the United Kingdom were unable to stop suicide bombers attacking public transport systems, it is therefore arguable that they and other Western countries are not ready for a sniper campaign either. Osama Bin Laden and his cohorts have certainly shown that they know how to switch their methods to ensure that they take the defenses by surprise.

Types of sniper threat

- **Professional sniper.** Well trained and disciplined; excellent shot.
- **Military trained.** Not a sniper, but trained soldier; adequate shot.
- **Irregular gunman**. Not so well trained; may have local knowledge and natural skill.
- **Criminal**. Possible military background; driving force is personal gain.
- **Terrorist**. Political or religious motivation; belief will dictate his/her determination; may have no interest in preserving own life.
- **Unhinged:** Irrational; almost impossible to predict; may be seeking publicity for personal grievance or looking for "death by cop" solution.

Much of the methodology of military sniping is common to all armies; most snipers are taught following approximately the same syllabus, and once in the field they face much the same problems. Therefore, on the battlefield, once an enemy sniper starts work it should not take too long for the counter-sniper cell to begin to develop some ideas as to what their quarry is up to and where he is likely to strike next. Away from the conventional battlefield, however, the counter-sniper cell has a much more severe problem: before ever reaching a shooting option against a terrorist sniper (or, as in the case of the Washington Beltway Snipers, simple criminals) the cell must first work out what their enemy is trying to achieve and how well they are equipped to do it. It is only after working out what is important to the terrorist that the counter-terrorist cell can begin to discover weaknesses that might then be exploited.

One example was when the British infantry deployed to Sarajevo in Bosnia in 1996 as part of a United Nations peacekeeping operation and were plagued by snipers engaging both them and civilians on an almost daily basis. By careful analysis of the tactics, times, and bullet trajectories, the counter-sniper coordinator was able to pinpoint the source of the shooting and then, in a two-pronged attack, remove the threat. This was achieved by first identifying the specific apartment in a high-rise building that the snipers were using, and then having British snipers ready to return fire the instant the enemy engaged. The second prong involved the battalion machine gun platoon: once the British snipers opened fire the machine gunners, having carefully calculated

ABOVE: The thought of going into a large industrial building to flush out a routed sniper is not a pleasant one. Here Finnish soldiers cautiously move around a disused factory during counter-sniper training.

BELOW: These Finnish soldiers cover every movement of each other around the building, but they cannot cover all angles; in any event at this stage a sensible sniper has already left.

ABOVE: Moving from one floor to another on the hunt for a concealed or cornered sniper is a very risky business, as illustrated by the intense look on this Finnish soldier's face, even though this is only training.

how long it would take for the enemy to retreat to the stairways at the rear of the building, engaged the stairways with a hail of automatic fire, which successfully caught the retreating gunmen. Not surprisingly, all sniper attacks on British troops in this area quickly stopped. This was an excellent example of the counter-sniper coordinator using his experience to put himself in the attacker's shoes, identify the tactics being used, identify the weak point, and then lead the enemy into an ambush from which there was no escape.

Principles

Out-think your enemy. Many centuries ago, the Chinese strategist/philosopher Sun Tsu advised that "those who understand the

ABOVE: British and Ukrainian snipers exchange rifles and familiarize themselves with each other's equipment. Such opportunities should always be taken up by the professional sniper.

enemy never suffer defeat," and this remains as true today as it was then. Thus, in order to counter any type of sniper threat (or threat in general for that matter) the essential first step is to study the enemy in detail to determine his or her likely thought-processes, as well as what experience and training they may have

ABOVE: British and Belgian para commandos exchange ideas and thoughts on sniping while cross-training during a UN operation. The Belgian commando is lying behind the British AI sniper rifle.

BELOW: The author recently arranged a sniper seminar in Pristina, Kosovo, for all UN snipers in country, and each unit set up a display to familiarize themselves with each other's equipment.

had, and what tactics they may have been had, and what tactics they may have been taught. There are many ways in which to out-think and defeat a sniper, but since this book is not intended to be a training manual for would-be terrorists it will only highlight the major issues in the complex, detailed, and demanding world of counter-sniping. The first aspect in any operation will be Time.

Factors affecting counter-sniper planning

- Threat groups.
- Enemy modus operandi.
- Enemy religion/beliefs/habits.
- Enemy weapon availability and capabilities.
- Enemy levels of training/competence.
- Enemy desire to succeed.
- Enemy mental approach to mission.
- History of previous enemy threat/operations.
- Does the enemy consider civilian casualties?
- Time available to enemy.
- Time available to you.

Time. This is a major determinant in deciding how any military or police task is to be approached; if it is limited, then the counter-sniper may well be forced into taking shortcuts that are better avoided, although the urgency of the mission—if, for example, lives are in imminent danger—may dictate otherwise. It is for this reason that contingency planning is so essential, because it means that dozens, maybe even hundreds,

of possible scenarios are established and analyzed in peacetime, and countermeasures are devised and practiced and, where necessary, modified. It does not necessarily follow that the actual situations that arise will fit in with any one of these contingency plans, but it should be possible to "cherry-pick" elements from various plans. Western security forces are, in general, excellent at training for and actually conducting attacks, but the societies they seek to defend are increasingly at the mercy of a dedicated enemy who is able to choose the time and place of his attacks. Some of these terrorist operations may be frustrated, but such a victory usually rates very low for media interest, whereas every successful terrorist attack gets the widest possible exposure.

The enemy. The predominant factor in any counter-terrorist/counter-sniper operation is the adversary, and a logical starting point is the human element of the problem. The personality and ethnic and national backgrounds will all have to be examined as all can have a significant impact on the counter-sniper plan. It could well be that normal drills or Standard Operating Procedures (SOPs) have to be modified or even changed completely. For example, if a covert counter-sniper team were operating in an anti-terrorist role in a Western nation, their discovery by a passer-by or the media would compromise the mission, but would not automatically mean that they would be attacked; hence, a risk of detection can be accepted. There are, however, certain parts of the world where, if such a pair were to be discovered, they would be in great danger of being attacked and killed by the

Selection of sniper rifles known to have been used by terrorists

Type	Caliber	Origin	Where used
Dragunov	7.62 x 54 rimmed	USSR (Russia)	Middle East, Africa
Mosin Nagant	7.62 x 54 rimmed		Russia, Asia, Middle East
Lee Enfield	.303in	UK	Asia, Ireland, Africa
Barrett M82	.50 (12.7mm)	USA	UK
Ruger M77	7.62 x 51 NATO,	USA	Europe, Latin America, USA

civilian population. Such risks must be carefully assessed before deploying a counter-sniper team with limited back-up.

Herein lies the advantage in having a dedicated counter-sniper cell: it can conduct training, but is also able to research into potential enemies. Such assessments will include how the enemy thinks, what is important in their daily lives, and how they might react in various scenarios. These factors will be part of the jigsaw that will be assembled to form a coherent blueprint, which will then make it possible to devise a plan to counter them. Another part of the assessment is the study of previous attacks carried out by the potential enemy, although it must not be assumed that he, too, will not have studied his mistakes and learnt from them.

Weapons. Another aspect to be studied is the potential enemy's likely weapons, their type, how well they shoot, how well-balanced they are, and how suitable they would be for stalking over long distances. Further aspects to be studied include how easily they break down, how this affects the zeroing, what optics might be carried and their power and clarity of vision, and so on.

Dedication to task. The amount of effort a potential enemy is prepared to put into succeeding in his or her mission has a major effect on the counter-sniper's defensive options. An

LEFT: A French Foreign Legion sniper examines a Romanian SVD sniper rifle when the two meet at the French camp in Mitrovica, Kosovo. A British sniper is also present, indicated by the L96 sniper rifle being held by the Romanian.

enemy who has reasons to live and whose common-sense is stronger than his or her bravery is always easier to take on than someone who is actively seeking death. If time is taken to learn as much as possible about potential enemies, then a good understanding of their motivational focus, and hence their desired results of any attack, can be gauged. Armed with this information the counter-sniper cell can assess its own assets, their ability to deal with the problem should it arise, and what they need to improve their capability.

Establishing a counter-sniper option

One of the most important requirements of a dedicated counter-sniper force is a good intelligence system and a keen eye for finding out and recognizing what is of value and, of equal importance, what is not. The counter-sniper coordinator must identify every source open to him, starting by establishing working links to his own national military and law-enforcement intelligence units, which, apart from anything else, will enable the counter-sniper team to access intelligence-gathering means that far outreach their own budgetary restraints. It will also serve as a starting point for a working trust to be established between the unit and those it maybe called upon to assist, as well as those it may, itself, call upon for help.

Source identification. The traditional means of intelligence-gathering are well known, ranging from electronic (ELINT) to human (HUMINT) means, but there are many others. For example, open literature and, increasingly, the Internet contain vast amounts of information, as do international

Methods of limiting the sniper threat

- Body armor.
- Very obvious protection parties.
- Aggressive patrolling techniques.
- Dummy targets/doppelgänger/deception.
- Counter-snipers trained and available.
- Detailed counter-sniper study.
- Coordinated central counter-sniper cell.
- Visibility-reducing screens (natural/artificial).
- General awareness of population.
- Education of population.

BELOW: Large military displays are the perfect training tool in peacetime and a perfect target for the terrorist sniper with hostile intent.

military open days and trade shows. Advice and training gained from experts within the military and industry will go further to educate the counter-sniper on shot-placement and hence the weak areas, but getting the teams to visit and learn for themselves is an opportunity that should never be missed. Open days and displays are good ways of supplementing official visits and also serve to train and identify methods of attack for sniper/counter-sniper teams.

Types of counter-sniper options

Active: Sniper threat is already present and active.

Passive: Plans to counter or prevent a sniper threat from developing in the first place.

Indexing risk targets. In order to protect, a counter-sniper team must collate all the knowledge on potential enemies and use this to identify likely weak areas and targets to be considered for protective planning. On a national level this will include the country's infrastructure as well as individuals and key points. When looking at ordinary people and VIPs, their life-style, routine, routes, and places of residence must all be taken into consideration. When areas and routes have to be assessed, the use of panoramic photographs or low-level helicopter flight may assist in identifying a sniper footprint and hence likely firing points. Prior to any protective detail taking place, a commander and at least one other must spend time in the area, or on the routes to be taken, in order to build up local knowledge and a feel for the area, to establish for themselves a "pattern-of-life." This local knowledge will enable the counter-snipers to become alert to the "absence of the normal, presence of the abnormal" and so raise awareness to potential threats. Areas and buildings should be broken down into areas of responsibility and coded for quick and easy reference between counter-sniper teams and the Counter Assault Team (CAT).

Rules of engagement. A counter-sniper unit must have clear, unambiguous, and legally defined rules of engagement, to remove any hesitation in opening fire when it is necessary, and thus risking lives. The rules are also necessary to protect the sniper from prosecution during the after-action investigation, and to reduce the effects of the inevitable media interest. Failure to follow

Data required to indicate sniper pattern
- Time of day of attack.
- Area of sniper fire.
- Sightings of small units/individuals before or after incidents.
- Engagement range.
- Role of victim and his/her importance.
- Weather conditions at time of shot.
- Hit ratio.

Critical national infrastructure
Definition: " Large scale loss of life, serious impact on the economy, grave social consequences for the community and of immediate concern to the Government." This includes:
- Communications.
- Emergency services.
- Energy.
- Financial.
- Food.
- Government and public services.
- Public safety.
- Health.
- Transport.
- Water.

rules, and rules that are unclear, lead to recrimination when mistakes are made.

Standard Operating Procedures. It is essential that the counter-sniper commander establishes a set of SOPs that all his team members will follow, and that any associated friendly forces can be made aware of. This does not mean a clamp-down on individual initiative, but it is essential to ensure that for all perceived situations the teams know the drills they have to carry out and, in particular, that new recruits to the unit can study in order to master the drills he or she is expected to carry out.

Counter-sniper measures

The counter-sniper team will be called upon to provide advice on methods to be employed to reduce the threat of a sniper attack. In order to do this the team commander must be an experienced sniper himself, so that he can place himself in the enemy's position and plan the attack he is being asked to protect against. There will be a finite number of ways in which a sniper can carry out an attack, and his aim, desired effect, and readiness to be caught or killed will narrow the choices even further. Having taken all those into account, it may be that some very simple changes in the target's lifestyle or surroundings may be all that are required to deter the sniper, by making it impossible for him to engage.

A possible scenario

Just one scenario will illustrate the ease with which large-scale disruption could be caused by a coordinated sniper attack. Imagine that several, not just one, of the main feeder routes into a major city beltway or ring road were to be targeted by terrorist snipers. At a given time each sniper targets a large fuel- or passenger-carrying vehicle in rush-hour traffic, and kills the drivers, causing the vehicles to crash out of control, leading to serious vehicle accidents and blocking the traffic. The rush hour is a time when most police forces stay off the roads to avoid "police-induced" traffic jams, so that apart from the obvious carnage, an immediate buildup of grid-locked traffic rapidly spreads out around the whole city road system until all movement ceases. Police, fire, ambulance, and other emergency services will be heading out to what appears to be isolated vehicle accidents, because until gunshot is determined as the cause this is all that can be assumed, particularly if the attacks have been carried out in different police areas. The terrorists, who are all still in place or have moved to an alternative firing position, now engage the emergency services, killing as many as possible of those who arrive to assist the injured, before disappearing to safe houses or onto their next area of operation.

As it becomes obvious that the attacks have been coordinated and were terrorist-driven, the government comes under increasing pressure from the media and public in general, forcing it to spend huge amounts of money to track down the perpetrators and also attempt to prevent another attack. At a suitable time, the terrorists strike again, only this time hitting unlikely targets such as farmers, factory workers, and hospital staff. Next they move to the rail system and then back to everyday workers. Each attack is in a different area of the country and carried out by different shooters to maximize the effect and make it difficult for the police and security services to identify and apprehend the terrorists involved.

Such a scenario could happen in any

nation around the world and its success would depend upon the preparations of the country's police forces and the acceptance by politicians, police, and public alike that this is a real threat, and one for which plans must be made. Nor is such a multi-strike scenario a novel recipe for terrorists; such coordinated attacks, including snipers, have been used for many years, and Osama Bin Laden is by no means the only one to be aware of their uses. So far, terrorists have chosen to use bombs since these generate immediate media images to promote their cause, as in the case of the London attacks in 2005. That could change, however, and it is essential that preparations are made for other forms of attack. The security services must not allow themselves to be mesmerized by bombs, chemical agents, and other weapons of mass destruction (WMD), horrific as they may be, and

ignore the lesser possibility of the use of small arms against the innocent people of target nations.

Predicting terrorist targets

As with any military operation, a terrorist attack must, of necessity, be preceded by a period of intelligence-gathering, active planning, and the coordination of people and resources, all of which will have visible aspects to them and are identifiable if people know what to look for. The initial focus for the counter-sniper planner is the list of sniper-vulnerable targets, which will give

BELOW: Easily identifiable military transport just makes a terrorist's life that much simpler, as the British found out against the IRA. Military transport should blend in with the local transport to help protect off duty or unarmed soldiers.

him a limited, although perhaps not exhaustive, list of areas and subjects to be considered, and a list of staff and associated people to be educated and utilized in the task of denying the area to the terrorist.

Recently seized terrorist videotape shows the method and the detail with which the terrorists carry out their reconnaissance, and these tapes should be part of every police force's public education material. After all, one of the main ways PIRA operations were limited in British cities was the education of the public in what to look for, with advertisements and posters, coupled with the education of staff at likely targets. The more people who are aware of terrorist methods and what to look for, the harder it is for the terrorist to move and to set up attacks.

Once terrorists have selected a target, it becomes necessary for them to conduct detailed surveillance, which will be carried out by more than one person. The most obvious method will be by the discreet watching of a location and its day-to-day business, trying to identify a weakness in its defenses and daily procedures. This could be carried out by a couple sat on a public bench, for example, through to a member of the team securing a part-time job at the target. The methods are limited only by the attacker's imagination.

One activity which is of great help to the security services would be for staff and families at likely targets to be encouraged to keep a record, either written or audio, simply recording anything at all, however, seemingly innocent, that appears suspicious or simply outside the usual pattern. If potential targets or the people around them appear to be alert and aware of their surroundings, these acts alone tend to deter any potential intruder who is observing movement patterns. The terrorist observers could feel that they may have been identified, feel exposed, and look elsewhere. The target staff/families should be encouraged to be methodical in their observations, looking for any ground sign, disturbances such as crushed grass, broken foliage or discarded cigarette butts, which might indicate that someone has been present and possibly watching the daily routine around a residence or other site. Similarly, if vehicles seem to appear more frequently than the normal random pattern this, too, should be recorded. Two simple and well-proven methods for recording such important information are as follows:

For vehicles use the mnemonic—CRIMP, which means:

- **C**olor
- **R**egistration
- **I**dentifying features (anything obviously unusual such as repairs, rust, broken lights, sports wheels, stickers, racing stripes)
- **M**ake and **M**odel
- **P**eople

For people, the "A-to-H method" helps those involved remember what to look for and record:

- **A**ge
- **B**uild (heavy or slim; large, medium or small frame)
- **C**lothing description (color and type)
- **D**istinguishing features (scars, tattoos, spectacles, mannerisms)
- **E**levation (height)

- Facial features (beard, moustache, color of eyes, shape of nose, and teeth)
- Gait (the way the person walks; their stride)
- Hair (color and style)

Ways to reduce sniper options

Reduce the sniper's ability to:
- See.
- Move.
- Shoot.
- Use his/her initiative.
- Become offensive.

This can be achieved by:

- Screens.
- Net curtains.
- Tinted/reflective glass.
- Armored glass.
- Trees.
- Deception.
- Decoys.
- Overt patrolling.
- Surveillance systems (CCTV).
- Detailed planning.

Detection surveillance

- Look for the absence of the normal and the presence of the abnormal.
- People photographing or videoing key points or buildings.
- Repeated passes by the same vehicle.
- Repeated sightings of the same people.
- Repeated sightings of parked occupied vehicles.

The counter-sniper unit—equipment

It is a given that the counter-sniper unit should be a national body with standardized weapons and equipment, so that, wherever possible it and its members do not stand out from the average police or military unit. Unit peculiarities, badges, and special uniforms only serve to highlight the unit's presence to any watching terrorist and to the media; elite status comes from professionalism and by earning the respect of one's colleagues, not by a catchy patch, elaborate T-shirt or an aggressive and patronizing manner.

The unit must have equipment that is comparable and interoperable with that of units likely to be working alongside it in various scenarios. To that end such equipment as communications and battery-operated items should be of a common type of power supply in order to facilitate re-supply on elongated tasks.

Weapons. There will always be a debate about the relative merits of bolt-action and semi-automatic sniper rifles, and the only sensible option is for the counter-sniper team to have both types, so that its members can have the maximum operational flexibility. Obviously, counter-snipers must train for the longer-range shots, although it is a very brave officer who will authorize a shot of six hundred yards or more to be taken in an operational situation. That said, the counter-sniper team must also have, in addition to both bolt-action and semi-automatic weapons, a range of long barrel and short, concealable-barrel weapons to choose from. In some contemporary situations, in particular the terrorist problem, it is highly likely

that a second or even third rapid shot will be required, so it makes sense to include a semi-automatic sniper rifle in the team armory. The quality and accuracy of modern 5.56mm (.223-caliber) and 7.62mm (.308-caliber) sniper rifles mean they are more than suitable for the task. A logical and cost effective option would be to issue the observer in the pair the semi-automatic and so deploy with a flexible combination able to cover most scenarios. It is also important that the counter-sniper team is permanently issued with a range of appropriate weapons so that they can carry out continuous training on all types. Each of these weapons must have a sub-minute-of-angle accuracy and be rugged enough to hold its zero even after the harsh handling some deployment

ABOVE: A selection of the tools of the trade for the sniper: a wind meter, GPS, and mini saw to assist in the construction of concealed firing positions.

methods and situations may force upon the counter-snipers.

Ammunition. No matter how good the rifle, it is only as good as its ammunition. It is a very false economy to seek to save money by buying inferior or even standard-grade ammunition for counter-sniper teams who should be issued with match-grade ammunition appropriate to the various potential scenarios. To the non-specialist, all ammunition of a given type looks the same, but to the professional marksman there are minor, but highly significant, differences between each batch, resulting in variations in performance and requiring them to be test-fired and their precise characteristics recorded, a process known as "proofing." Such infinitesimal differences may also be very significant in legal proceedings that follow most counter-sniper operations, at least in Western countries.

RIGHT: The Leopold x40 spotting telescope.. Note the honeycombed kill-flash lens cover designed to stop the sun's rays reflecting off the lens and compromising the sniper.

BELOW: The Pilkington Kite sight, or Common Weapon Sight in British Army use. The CWS night sight works by gathering available light and amplifying it to produce an image.

High-power telescopic sight. As with ammunition, it follows that maximizing both the performance of the chosen weapon and the sniper's observational skills necessitates a suitable telescopic sight. The degree of magnification depends on projected roles; of course, the greater the magnification the greater the costs, but as the sniper spends most of his time observing and the legal requirement entails that the sniper must be 100 percent certain of his target identification, the sights must have high magnification as well as high optical quality. Thus, a telescopic sight of at least x10 power is needed, while most modern snipers adopt a variable power unit in the x3-x12 magnification

ABOVE: The Leopold x40 spotting scope comes with a padded cover that semi-camouflages as well as protects the scope, with easy-access zippered openings at the eye piece and a drop-down flap cover for the objective lens.

range, which allows them to zoom-in or -out and avoid eyestrain. The scope should have a minimum of a 50mm objective lens to maximize the light gathering capabilities for low-light observation and shooting. It should also be selected in conjunction with the planned image intensifying night sight the unit intends to use.

Spotting scope. The counter-sniper pair also has a requirement for a high-magnification

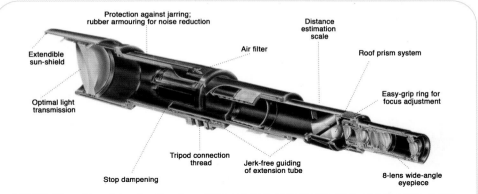

Protection against jarring;
rubber armouring for noise reduction

Distance
estimation
scale

Air filter

Roof prism system

Extendible
sun-shield

Easy-grip ring for
focus adjustment

Optimal light
transmission

Tripod connection
thread

Jerk-free guiding
of extension tube

Stop dampening

8-lens wide-angle
eyepiece

ABOVE: The older style of pull-out spotting scope is just as effective, and in some cases it can be stripped to clean the lenses. This allows the sniper to better understand the way the scope works, as he can actually see for himself the inner mechanism.

spotting scope for use by the observer to locate and identify targets for the sniper. This device should have the same graticule pattern as the sniper weapon scope to allow indication and joint distance estimation to take place as both members of the team are observing the same sight picture.

Binoculars/laser rangefinder. Some situations require hand-held binoculars rather than a larger spotting scope and it makes

sense to combine this with a laser rangefinder, which is normally binocular-based, anyway. It is also sensible to have the same graticule pattern etched onto the laser lenses, thus covering the possibility that the laser might fail or the battery give out. Such graticules would allow the sniper to fall back on the old-fashioned method of measuring and calculating distance using the mils and "known height" formula:

Range = known height x 1000 ÷ size in mils.

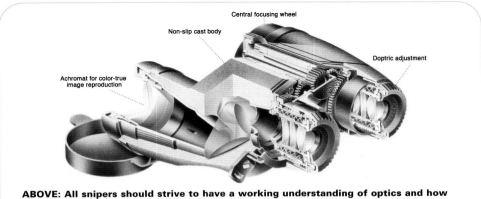

Central focusing wheel

Non-slip cast body

Doptric adjustment

Achromat for color-true
image reproduction

ABOVE: All snipers should strive to have a working understanding of optics and how they function. Exploded diagrams are a very good teaching vehicle and should be used where an optic cannot be stripped.

ABOVE: The very effective Leica Vector laser rangefinder binoculars and the Leopold x40 spotting scope in use by a British sniper.

Uniform. Very few manufacturers produce clothing and equipment, particularly for load-carrying, specifically for the sniper. Many seem to think that all that is required is a ghillie suit for rural operations, but this is only one element in the specialized camouflage needed by the sniper. Similarly, there will always be a need for load-carrying equipment, since the sniper team will deploy ready for extended operations and so will need various amounts and types of equipment, while not always having the luxury of a specific team vehicle.

ABOVE: The Leicas have a very sturdy, if somewhat heavy, tripod that provides the user with a very steady platform from which to observe.

LEFT: Thermal reduction has become a very important aspect for snipers with the increase in availability of thermal optical units. Issued to all British snipers, this thermal reduction suit consists of pants, smock, gloves, face veil, hood, and glasses that all work to reduce the sniper's thermal image.

RIGHT: A sniper pair demonstrating the effectiveness of the anti-thermal suit (although the obvious objective lenses would normally be covered).

Communications equipment. The counter-sniper team must have reliable and secure communications between themselves, their controlling officer, and their supporting unit if they are to be of any tactical use.

Command-and-control system. In hostage or terrorist scenarios where positive identification is essential, increasing numbers of sniper units are acquiring a special-to-role sniper control system. This comprises a series of remote cameras that attach to the sniper's sight and transmit the sight picture back to a central command screen, usually laptop-based, thus enabling the commander to see exactly the same picture as that presented to his firers. As a result, quick and accurate decisions to fire can be given. This also allows for easier control by the commander, who may have to coordinate a multiple target shoot simultaneously.

ABOVE: Another effective way to reduce thermal signature recognition is to masquerade as nature itself, covering body and equipment with natural vegetation.

BELOW: The reality of counter-sniping: an experienced sniper at a desk monitoring long gun activity and looking for the obvious build-up of a pattern that would indicate the attentions of a dedicated sniper.

Two such systems are the KAPPA (referred to in Chapter Three) and the Israeli-made HeloPoint "Snipco." The "Snipco" is a camera-based system that enables the sight picture presented to each sniper to be transmitted by radio link to the overall commander. It comprises three types of unit, the basic one being the individual camera, either mono or colored, with the necessary adapter, which is fitted to the telescopic sights of each sniper's weapon. The

ABOVE: The CastFire Solutions riflescope Eye-Cam with RF transmitter that can allow both sniper and controller to see the same real-time target image.

BELOW: A small personal role radio (PRR) that allows communications between individual soldiers and their command structure.

second unit is the transmission device, operating in either L- or S-band, with an antenna and a battery pack, which operates for four hours on one charge. The command

receiver unit uses a laptop with a 15-inch LCD display, which can present the commander with up to four snipers' views on a split screen, or a single sniper's view on a full screen. Full recording facilities are provided and the unit can also be linked via the Internet to authorized users anywhere in the world, using an on-line encryption system.

ABOVE: The German Army night sight fitted on a forward Picatinny rail to the G22 rifle.

RIGHT: The hand-held Lion thermal optic of the French Foreign Legion being tested by a British sniper looking to perfect ways of defeating its capabilities.

BELOW: A British issue telescopic sight cover is fitted to protect the equipment from the elements.

Night-viewing devices. There are numerous night-viewing devices available, generally of two types. One attaches directly to the front of the sniper's telescopic sight, usually mounted on a forward Picatinny rail (a standardized bracket used on firearms to provide a platform for accessories such as telescopic sights, lights, and lasers), or the unit may "piggy-back" the telescopic sight with prism attachments fitted onto the optical lens. A typical night-viewing device is the Simrad KN200/250, a third generation optical device which clips to the top of the rifle scope and by means of a vision splitter presents the sniper with a night capability through his normal rifle-mounted sniper scope. The system is bore-sighted to the rifle and then adjusted by simple focus and gain controls to achieve the optimum view for the prevailing weather and light conditions. The

focus range is from twenty-five yards to infinity, and the field-of-view varies from 10 to 12 degrees depending on the model. Battery life is approximately forty hours.

ABOVE: The Simrad Optronics KN 203 FAB night vision add-on sight can be fitted to a daylight telescope, allowing it to be moved between different weapon platforms without adjustment.

BELOW: The TAM-14 thermal monocular produced by Nivisys Industries can be hand-held, head/helmet-mounted, or weapon-mounted. It features white/hot or black/hot selection, eight-level contrast setting, and 2X digital zoom.

BELOW: The German Army night optical sight unit fitted to the G22. Note the rubber interface between the sight and the telescopic sight objective lens to form a light-proof seal between the two units.

ABOVE: The Nivisys Industries NADS-750 is a night-augmented day sight that can be clipped onto the sniper's dedicated day sight so that he does not have to remove the day sight to gain a night engagement capability, or change his standard aim posture.

Target indication. It is vital that any counter-sniper team can pass an accurate and easily understood target indication between different members of the same team, between teams or from the team to the commander. This requires a uniform identification system, and many sniper and assault units use a system in which the target is broken down into respective sides that are either numbered or color-coded in a clockwise direction. To break it down further, windows and doors can be key-coded according to floor and position on the floor, with a grid system covering windows across each floor and floors. Precisely how the system is set out does not really matter provided it is described in SOPs and all those involved use it properly. Thus, for example, in a system where the floors are numbered from ground upwards and doors/windows left to right, the number "3-5" would lead all snipers to the third floor and the fifth window from the left. A further refinement is that in a specific incident suspect target individuals can be assigned code- or nicknames to achieve brevity and speed up response times.

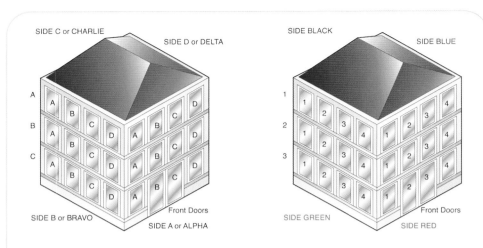

ABOVE: In an urban hostage situation each building will be broken down into color codes or letter/number codes to clarify the indication of events and targets to the snipers.

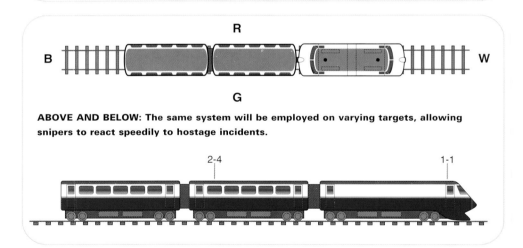

ABOVE AND BELOW: The same system will be employed on varying targets, allowing snipers to react speedily to hostage incidents.

Summary

Counter-sniping is an often-overlooked aspect of the sniper's trade. Many in authority take the view that if a person is trained as a sniper then he must automatically become a counter-sniper asset, as well. However, counter-sniping is a very specialized activity, being a varied and time-consuming area of operations that depends on full cooperation of all law enforcement departments and of military units to ensure that all available intelligence reaches the right desks. The whole scene is encapsulated in the adage that a counter-sniper must "out-think his enemy in order to outlive him." Two real-world examples now follow. First is the Washington, D.C., Beltway Sniper episode in which, while the perpetrators were eventu-

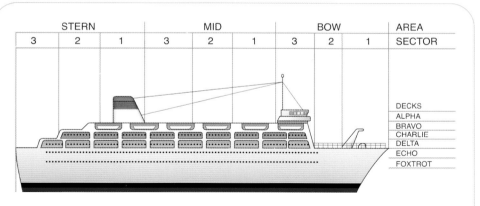

STERN			MID			BOW			AREA
3	2	1	3	2	1	3	2	1	SECTOR

DECKS
ALPHA
BRAVO
CHARLIE
DELTA
ECHO
FOXTROT

ABOVE: The target identification system can be applied to a cruise liner as easily as to an aircraft, train or building.

ally caught, it was not through a counter-sniper option, while the second shows just how a counter-sniper team can play a key role in a successful outcome.

THE WASHINGTON, D.C., "BELTWAY SNIPER" ATTACKS

At 10:30 PM on Thursday, September 5, 2002, Paul LaRuffa, owner of a small pizzeria in Clinton, Maryland, locked up his business after a successful day, and was walking towards his car when he was hit by five high-velocity bullets. He fell to the ground and was robbed of his day's earnings and a laptop computer, becoming the first known victim, albeit not fatal, of the two snipers who terrorized the Washington area for the next six weeks. These two men, John Allen Muhammad, 43, and Lee Boyd Malvo, 18, had spent time training in isolated areas on the U.S./Canadian border, where they prepared themselves for their sniper campaign against the people of the United States. On leaving there, they are believed to have worked their way down the Western seaboard, across the southern states and then up to the Washington, D.C., area, murdering and robbing along their route, although the full tally of these crimes may never be known. There followed a series of murders and attempted murders in and around D.C.—see table—which brought terror to the streets of the capital city before good police work, dedicated vigilance, and the brave actions of a truck driver brought about their arrest.

Muhammad and Malvo targeted the main areas of day-to-day activity, knowing that their actions would affect trade, economy, freedom of movement, and morale, and would lead to a huge outcry among the media and general public, who would be demanding that "something must be done." They assumed, quite correctly, that publicly elected officials would fear a backlash and apply additional pressure on the law-enforcement community to get a quick result, thus creating even greater chances of mistakes and oversights.

The Washington, D.C., Beltway Sniper Attacks: September 5 – October 24, 2002

Date (all 2002)	Place	Victim	Event	Comment
September 5 10:30 PM	Clinton, Maryland	Paul LaRuffa, 55, pizzeria owner	Shot fiive times at close range; wounded but survives	
September 21	Montgomery, Alabama	Claudine Parker, liquor store clerk	Shot and killed during robbery. A co-worker is wounded	
October 2 5:20 PM	Aspen Hill, Maryland		Shot fired through store window; no injuries	
October 2 6:05 PM	Wheaton, Maryland.	James Martin, 55, program analyst	Shot and killed in grocery store parking lot	First Beltway-area shooting
October 3 7:41 AM	Rockville, Maryland	James L. Buchanan, 39, landscaper	Shot and killed while mowing the grass at an auto mall	
October 3 8:12 AM	Aspen Hill, Maryland	Premkumar Walekar, 54, part-time taxi driver	Shot and killed while pumping gasoline into his taxi	
October 3 8:37 AM	Aspen Hill, Maryland	Sarah Ramos, 34, babysitter/housekeeper	Shot and killed while reading a book on a park bench	
October 3 9:58 AM	Kensington, Maryland	Lori Ann Lewis-Rivera, 25, nanny	Shot and killed while pumping gasoline at a Shell station	
October 3 9:15 PM	Kalmia Road, in Washington, D.C.	Pascal Charlot, 72, retired carpenter	Shot while walking; dies one hour later.	
October 4 2:30 PM	Fredericksburg, Virginia	Caroline Seawell, 43, mother	Shot loading groceries into van; wounded	
October 7 8:09 AM	Bowie, Maryland	Iran Brown, 13, schoolboy	Shot arriving at school; wounded	Name revealed later
October 9 8:18 PM	Near Manassas, Prince William County, Virginia	Dean Harold Meyers, 53, civil engineer, Vietnam veteran	Shot and killed while pumping gasoline at a Shell station	
October 11 9:30 AM	Near Fredericksburg, Spotsylvania	Kenneth Bridges, 53, businessman	Shot and killed while pumping gasoline at Exxon station	
October 14 9:15 PM	Outside Falls Church, Fairfax	Linda Franklin, 47, FBI intelligence analyst	Shot and killed outside store	Police receive lead; later proved to be false
October 19 8:00 PM	Ashland, Virginia	Jeffrey Hopper, 37, chief information officer, brokerage company	Shot in parking lot near steak-house; badly wounded but survives	Authorities discover a three-page letter from the shooter in the woods
October 21	Aspen Hill, Maryland		Richmond-area police arrest two men outside a gas station	Illegal immigrants unconnect-ed to the shooter
October 22 5:56 AM		Conrad Johnson, bus driver	Shot and killed on steps of his bus; dies next day	Shooter statement: "Your children are not safe, anywhere, at any time."
October 24			John Allen Muhammad, Lee Boyd Malvo arrested aleep in their automobile	Later convicted

The attacks were carried out with a Bushmaster .223-caliber XM-15 semi-automatic rifle, usually at a relatively short range, typically between fifty and about a hundred and fifty yards, fired from inside the trunk of a Chevrolet Caprice. The use of a motor vehicle in such circumstances is not new to the security services of the U.K.: at one stage in the Northern Ireland campaign the PIRA used a Mazda 626 as a firing platform for sniper attacks against police and army units, using a .50-caliber "Light-Fifty." Muhammad drilled a small and inconspicuous hole in the sill, so that the shooter, usually Malvo, could aim and fire the rifle from the prone position inside the car. The pair also regularly sent cryptic messages to the police to taunt them and goad them into over-reacting.

Their targets centered on what they saw as the "enemy infrastructure," such as fuel, food, general supplies, and movement, in order to lower morale and induce political bickering. Thus, by targeting gasoline stations, they forced many people to stay at home. When many citizens switched to public transportation, Muhammad and Malvo responded by shooting a bus driver, thus broadcasting a clear message that even bus travel was unsafe. They also targeted small convenience stores and the multitude of shopping malls where the majority of Americans do the bulk of their shopping. The snipers' intention was to restrict the average American's freedom of movement. To add to the feeling of menace they did not confine their targets to any one group in the

BELOW: The Washington "Beltway snipers" used a small 5.56mm/.223-caliber assault rifle and carried it around in a small duffel bag, with the weapon stripped into its two main component parts.

community. Thus, their victims ranged in age from thirteen to seventy-two; the ethnic grouping included black, white, and Asian; and there was an almost equal balance between men and women. In fact, whether intentionally or not, they targeted a complete cross-section of the community, thus ensuring that nobody could feel safe or immune from attack.

Their attacks seem to have been planned with military precision, even to the extent of heading in the opposite direction to the traffic-flow at a given time of the day, or driving away from the expected route of police

response units responding to the 911 call, to ensure they were never caught in a police cordon. The selection of an almost unknown type of firing platform, the elderly Chevrolet Caprice, was another well-planned tactic, and when the media foolishly published news that a "white van" was being used, not only did

BELOW: The modification to the old Chevy Caprice vehicle made it possible to move from within the vehicle into the trunk area by means of a hinged rear seat, and then to set up and fire through a cut-out in the rear section of the bodywork. With the lid almost down and the inner surface painted dark blue, the "Beltway sniper" pair were able to shoot without giving away their position.

every white van come under suspicion but the pair took further advantage by ensuring a white van was in the vicinity before shooting—not a difficult task, considering the proliferation of such vans in the United States. The pair also returned to the police cordon on more than one occasion so as to listen to police conversations and opinions, which enabled them to modify their *modus operandi* to take account of changes or perceived weaknesses in police tactics.

Their selection of targets appeared so random that it was very difficult for a police officer or federal agent without sniper experience to pick up any patterns. The pair were also well aware of the limitations of the local area police units and used these shortcomings against them. But, like the vast majority of criminals, Muhammad and Malvo kept going for just too long and were eventually caught through a combination of police doggedness and public awareness.

AIR FRANCE FLIGHT 8969

On December 24, 1994, four members of a fanatical Islamist group bluffed their way aboard Air France Flight 8969, which was about to depart Boumedienne International Airport in Algiers for Paris, France. The aircraft was an Airbus A300 with a crew of twelve and 224 passengers, while the terrorist unit comprised four men armed with a Kalashnikov assault rifle, a Uzi submachine gun, two pistols, and a quantity of explosives and detonators. The terrorists took control on the ground and quickly showed that they meant business by killing one of the passengers and throwing his body onto the tarmac. The response in both Algeria and France was

excellent, with government ministers, airline and airport officials, and counter-terrorist units all assembling quickly. Negotiators managed to obtain the release of some sixty-three women and children, but there was a problem because the hard-line commander of the Algerian Special Forces unit surrounding the Airbus refused to allow the airliner to depart for France, whereupon a second hostage, a Vietnamese diplomat, was killed and his body thrown to the ground. The impasse with the Algerian Special Forces continued until a third hostage was killed, and the commander was finally compelled by his government to give way and the aircraft departed, supposedly for Paris, at 0200 December 26.

The French counter-terrorist squad from *Groupe d'Intervention de la Gendarmerie Nationale* (GIGN) tried to fly to Algiers but were refused permission to land so they diverted to a Spanish airport, where they spent some time on the ground before flying to Marseille-Marignane, arriving just before the hijacked Airbus, which had been diverted from its flight to Paris, because, so the hijackers were told, it needed to refuel. Once on French soil GIGN attempted to negotiate with the hijackers while concurrently deploying snipers who kept the aircraft under intense observation, trying to work out where the hijackers were and what they were planning to do. This phase lasted some fourteen hours, during which the negotiators managed to persuade the hijackers to allow a party on board to clean the toilets and bring food, and after that to move the passengers to the rear of the main cabin.

Late in the afternoon of December 26, an assault was about to be launched when the aircraft suddenly moved closer to the control tower and GIGN had to move all its troops to new positions. A terrorist then fired at the control tower, unwittingly giving the OK for the assault. The French Special Forces attacked through several of the aircraft doors while GIGN snipers on the roof of the control tower using 0.50-caliber rifles fired on the terrorists on the flight deck through the cockpit windows. Despite the notorious difficulties of such "through-glass" shots, they killed some of the terrorists but avoided hitting the pilot, co-pilot and navigator who were lying on the cockpit floor. There was an intense gun battle inside the aircraft, where some GIGN gendarmes fought the terrorists while others got the passengers off the aircraft as quickly as they could. The operation ended with all four terrorists dead, while three passengers were killed by the terrorists. Astonishingly, although several GIGN and passengers were wounded in the gun battle, none of these was killed. Among the key elements in this incident were the GIGN snipers whose trained observation gave the GIGN commander a very good idea of what was going on aboard the aircraft, while their shooting during the assault kept the terrorists pinned down and also killed some of them.

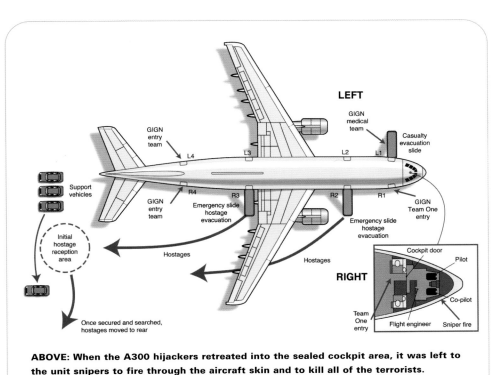

ABOVE: When the A300 hijackers retreated into the sealed cockpit area, it was left to the unit snipers to fire through the aircraft skin and to kill all of the terrorists.

CHAPTER 7 SNIPER WEAPONS

There is a large and ever-increasing choice of sniper rifles available today and there is space here only to describe the capabilities of a selection of, first, the most common and, second, some of the newer models that have only recently arrived on the market. One of the most notable recent developments is the rapid increase in the number and use of the .50-caliber weapons, usually known outside the United States as 12.7mm caliber. These weapons make it possible to engage and hit a man-sized target at over two thousand five hundred yards, while a large number of air, land and sea weapons and other equipment can also be engaged by them. This has strengthened the sniper's role on the battle-

field, since he now has the ability to seriously damage, if not actually destroy, almost anything, including an armored vehicle, provided he is correctly sited and supported.

Worryingly, for counter-terrorist units, this proliferation in models available and the increase in caliber have also added another deadly weapon system to the terrorist arsenal. For example, the recent sale of some two thousand 12.7mm sniper rifles by Austrian arms manufacturer Steyr to the Iranian Border Police has caused considerable concern amongst the United States and other Western governments, because there is a very real fear that they may be passed on to terrorists. Indeed, the use of .50-caliber weapons by terrorists is not new; the Provisional Irish Republican Army (PIRA) used a Barrett .50-caliber anti-materiel rifle against the British Army in a well-publicized campaign in the 1990s, while numerous home-made and nationally produced .50-caliber rifles were used throughout the Bosnia and Kosovo operations by all sides.

Austria: Steyr-Mannlicher IWS 2000

The Austrian arms company, Steyr-Mannlicher, has ventured into the world of the large caliber rifle with its IWS 2000 (IWS = Individual Weapons System), which is also described as an anti-materiel rifle (AMR). The weapon fires a 15.2mm Special APFSDS (Armor-Piercing Fin-Stabilized Discarding Sabot) round through a smooth-

LEFT: A French Special Forces soldier practicing a modified version of the alternate laid-back position with a PGM sniper rifle with a fully suppressed barrel. Other barrels are available for this excellent little rifle.

bore (i.e., unrifled) barrel. This round is slightly larger than the commonly used .50BMG (Browning Machine Gun) (12.7mm), but has now been surpassed, for shoulder-held weapons, by the 20mm round used in several of the weapons described below. The IWS 2000 and its round are designed to destroy anything on the battlefield except for a main battle tank and have been developed into an extremely destructive weapons system. The 308-grain APFSDS tungsten dart will penetrate nearly two inches (40mm) of rolled homogenous armor at 1,093 yards (1,000m) and is reported to be capable of going through the side armor of any modern infantry fighting vehicle (IFV).

Data
Model: Steyr IWS 2000 AMR
Caliber: 15.2mm (.598-inch)
Muzzle velocity: 4,757ft/sec (1,450m/sec)
Weight: 39.7lb (18kg)
Barrel: 47.25 inches (1,200mm)
Magazine: Five rounds

Austria: Steyr-Mannlicher .50 HS

The latest .50-caliber rifle from Steyr-Mannlicher is the single-shot HS rifle, which has a manually operated rotating bolt, adjustable cheek-piece, and a permanently fitted MILSTD (military standard) Picatinny rail for fitting a telescopic sight. The barrel is partially fluted, and is fitted with a large and effective muzzle-brake. The weapon has been available since 2004, and has added another option to the market for the ever-growing .50-caliber operator club. One thousand of these rifles were sold to the Iranian Border

Guard, supposedly for their protection against trans-border criminals.

ABOVE: The Steyr-Mannlicher .50-caliber HS recently sold to Iran against the wishes of many of the West's governments. There are now very real fears that some of these rifles will find their way to terrorists and insurgents in Iraq.

Data
Model: Steyr-Mannlicher .50 HS
Caliber: .50BMG or .460 Steyr
Muzzle velocity: n.k.
Weight: 27.3lb (12.4kg)
Barrel: 33.0 inches (833mm)
Magazine: Single shot; no magazine

France: PGM Commando/Hecate

The PGM family of weapons is manufactured by PGM Precision, and is marketed worldwide by the famous company Fabrique Nationale (FN) of Herstal, Belgium, and its subsidiaries. All have a high-grade alloy skeletal stock and are designed to be both lightweight and easily transportable; their users agree that they are very accurate and well-balanced. The Commando versions have a quick-change barrel facility that enables the weapon to take the standard 18-inch barrel or a 23-inch or suppressed barrel depending

upon the unit mission and situation, which is a very useful option for clandestine missions. The Hecate version is basically a larger caliber version of the same basic design, chambered for the .50BMG round, which places it in the heavy rifle bracket. It is a very good and accurate weapon, and a welcome addition to any armory.

Data
Model: PGM Commando
Caliber: 7.62 x 51mm NATO
Muzzle velocity: 950ft/sec (290m/sec)
Weight: 12.lb (5.5kg)
Barrel: Three variations (see text)
Magazine: Five rounds

Model: PGM Hecate
Caliber: .50inBMG (12.7 x 99mm)
Muzzle velocity: 2,705ft/sec (825m/sec)
Weight: 30.4lb (13.8kg)
Barrel: 27.5 inches (700mm)
Magazine: Seven rounds

Germany: Heckler & Koch MSG-90

The MSG-90 is the military development of the PSG 1, both of which are descended from the company's world-famous G3 self-loading rifle. The German abbreviation MSG stands for *"Militärisches Scharfschützen Gewehr,"* which translates as "military sharpshooter (i.e., sniper) rifle" while the figure "90" indicates the year in

LEFT: The fully suppressed PGM Commando sniper rifle with the basic equipment issued to French military snipers, including laser rangefinder, binoculars, side arm, spotting scope, and spare un-suppressed barrel.

ABOVE: A French Army sniper team practicing with the .50-caliber Hecate sniper rifle. The Hecate is a very accurate and reliable rifle that has seen action with the French forces around the world.

ABOVE: The author on attachment to the U.S. Marines at Quantico test-firing the HK MSG-90 sniper rifle, which at the time was being considered with the SR25 as the new designated marksman rifle. As it was, both rifles lost out to an updated version of the M21.

BELOW: A Royal Marines commando test-fires the same rifle, with U.S. Marines watching in the background.

which it entered production. It is a very robust weapon and uses a semi-automatic action. It is one of a number of modern self-loading sniper rifles currently available; indeed, there are a number of sniper scenarios where the rapid delivery of a second and third shot is required, for which these, rather than bolt-action, rifles are the most suitable.

Data
Model: Heckler & Koch MSG-90
Caliber: 7.62 x 51mm NATO
Muzzle velocity: 2,788ft/sec (850m/sec)
Weight: 14.1lb (6.4kg)
Barrel: 23.6 inches (600mm); four grooves; right-hand twist
Magazine: Five or twenty rounds

ABOVE: The French .50-caliber Hecate sniper rifle has proven to be a very reliable and accurate weapon, seen here in the hands of a British sniper during a familiarization range day. The weapon came very close to being issued to the British Army but ultimately lost out to the AI .338-caliber rifle.

Hungary: Gepard M1

Hungary was one of the first of the former Warsaw Pact countries to enter the .50-caliber rifle market with both the M1 (single shot) and M2 (semi-automatic) rifles which are chambered for the U.S. .50inBMG (12.7 x 99mm) or, with a different barrel, the Russian 12.7 x 108mm round. These two were followed by the M3, a modified and heavier version of the M2, which was chambered for the even larger 14.5 x 114mm round. This round dates back to World War II and was originally designed for use in anti-aircraft machine guns; its use in this rifle made it among the most powerful ever used in a shoulder-fired weapon up to that time. All these weapons are capable of penetrating about an inch (25mm) of armor

Data (M1 only)
Model: Hungarian State Arsenals M1
Caliber: 0.50inBMG (12.7 x 99mm) or Russian 12.7 x 108mm.
Muzzle velocity: 2,822ft/sec (860m/sec)
Weight: 38.6lb (17.5kg)
Barrel: 43.3 inches (1,100mm)
Magazine: Single-shot; no magazine

at over 600 yards and pose a serious anti-materiel and anti-personnel threat.

Russian Federation: Dragunov SVD

Designed by Yevgeniy Dragunov and produced at the Soviet state arsenal at Izhevsk, the *Snayperskaya Vintovka Dragunova* (SVD) entered service with the Soviet Army in 1967 as its standard sniper rifle, being carried by one man in each rifle platoon. It became the standard sniper rifle of all Warsaw Pact armies, as well as of many of the former Soviet Union's allies, and was also built under license in Bulgaria, China, Egypt, Hungary, Iraq, and Romania. All those who have fired it agree that it is an accurate, comfortable and well-balanced rifle to use. It was one of the first semi-automatic rifles for snipers but has a very short piston

BELOW: The Gepard .50-caliber rifle was one of many such rifles to be produced and extensively used throughout the Balkans conflicts. Its design, and that of many others, has much in common with the World War II anti-tank rifles and can be a deadly weapon with the right ammunition and a well trained crew.

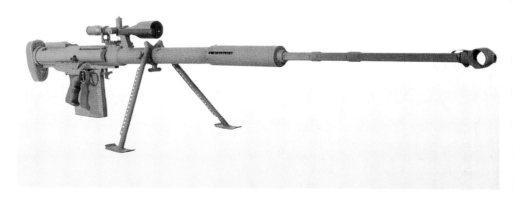

stroke to avoid upsetting the firer's point-of-aim. The rifle has been updated in several countries, but the basic original is still in use and all versions remain very effective today. The prospect of such a weapon being increasingly available to terrorists is worrying.

Data

Model: Dragunov SVD

Caliber: 7.62 x 54R rimmed

Muzzle velocity: 2,723ft/sec (830m/sec)

Weight: 9.5lb (4.3 kg)

Barrel: 24.5 inches (622mm); four grooves; right-hand twist; one turn in 10 inches (254mm)

Magazine: Ten rounds

Russian Federation: VSS Silent Sniper Rifle

The Russian *Vinovka Snaiperskaja Spetsialnaya* (= special sniper rifle) was intended to replace silenced weapons then in service with *Spetsnaz* and other Soviet-era special forces. It was built to fire a new, heavy, sub-sonic 9 x 39mm round, which was required to penetrate the body armor then being increasingly used by NATO forces. It is widely used among Russian forces, particularly in Chechnya, where it is used for single-shot silent assassination and guard removal. Maximum effective range is shorter than many sniper rifles: 440 yards (400m) by day and 330 yards (300m) by night. As its name implies, it has a very

ABOVE: While being replaced by updated versions and different weapons in Russian service, the older SVD Dragunov rifles continue to surface in the hands of insurgents and terrorists. Here a British sniper familiarizes himself with it during cross-training with Ukrainian snipers.

RIGHT: The .50BMG-caliber AI AS50 is a semi-automatic, anti-materiel sniper rifle being developed for the U.S. Navy SEALs. Barrel, 27.25in stainless steel free-floating, one twist in 15in; weight, 31lb; magazine, 5-round box.

effective silencer, which must be fitted whenever the weapon is fired. The VSS was developed in tandem with the Silent Assault Rifle and is designed to be stripped down and carried in a concealed manner, being reassembled just prior to use.

Data
Model: VSS Silent Sniper Rifle
Caliber: 9 x 39mm
Muzzle velocity: Approx 1,080ft/sec (290m/sec)
Weight: 5.7lb (2.6 kg) empty; 7.5lb (3.41kg) loaded, with scope.
Barrel: 8.0 inches (200mm)
Magazine: Ten or twenty rounds in polymer box

South Africa: Mechem NTW-20

The availability of the large Russian 14.5 x 114mm round led the South African company Aerotek into designing a bolt-action rifle to fire this cartridge, resulting in a devastating sniper weapon with an effective range up to 2,500 yards (2,300m)—perhaps even beyond that, in the right hands. They then took the process one stage further to produce a similar weapon but this time chambered for the even larger and heavier 20 x 83.5mm MG151 round, which had been designed by the Germans in World War II for aircraft-mounted machine guns. The two weapons differ only in the barrel, bolt, and magazine, the remainder being common to both. The design includes an artillery-style recuperator system that reduces recoil for the firer to that of a Super-Magnum rifle. On operations these rifles can be stripped down into two parts for ease of transportation by a two-man team. The original design was by the Aerotek company, but this has since been bought out by the Mechem Division of the South African Denel Corporation.

Data (for 20mm version)
Model: Mechem NTW-20
Caliber: 20 x 83.5mm MG151
Muzzle velocity: 2,362ft/sec (720m/sec)
Weight: 62lb (28kg)
Magazine: Three-round box

United Kingdom: Accuracy International Model AW

Accuracy International (AI) is a British company established in the 1980s to design and manufacture very specialized and highly accurate, bolt-operated rifles. Its first design, known as the "Model PM," was accepted into British service in 1986 and issued to the army (infantry and Special Forces) and to the Royal Marines, who have used it operationally around the world since that date under the designation

Data
Model: Accuracy International AW
Caliber: 7.62 x 51mm NATO
Muzzle velocity: 2,756ft/sec (840m/sec); covert version 1,033ft/sec (315m/sec)
Weight: 14.33lb (6.5kg).
Barrel: 25.78 inches (655mm); four grooves, right-hand twist; one turn in 12 inches (305mm)
Magazine: Ten rounds

L96A1. It was modified slightly and then became the Model AW (= arctic warfare), although it is, in fact, used in all climates. It has also been sold to the armed forces of many

ABOVE: The G22 version of the Accuracy International AW rifle, modified for German Army service.

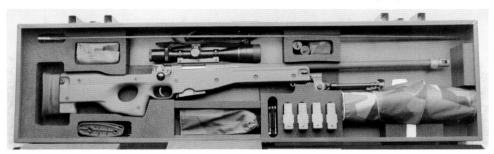

ABOVE: The AW version in its transit case with Swedish camouflage weapon cover under the barrel.

ABOVE: The AW with a screw-on tactical suppressor fitted to the end of its barrel.

ABOVE: AI also produce a fully suppressed sniper rifle with full-length suppressor and a much shorter barrel.

ABOVE: The AI .50-caliber bolt-action rifle that has seen operational success in Afghanistan and Iraq.

friendly countries; in the German Army, for example, it is known as the G22. The weapon is available with either a one-piece or a folding two-piece stock, and can be fully suppressed or fitted with a screw-on tactical suppressor.

United Kingdom: Accuracy International Model .338 Super Magnum

The Model .338 SM was developed by Accuracy International as a long-range, larger-caliber version of the Model AW, chambered for the .338 Lapua round. It was tested and then accepted by the British Army, with whom it is in service as the L115A1, and used as either a sniper rifle or as a "platoon-level support weapon." The rifle has a very high muzzle velocity, flat trajectory, and long range, and is a very easy weapon to fire. It has virtually the same range as .50-caliber weapons, although not quite the same heavy punch as the larger round.

Data
Model: Accuracy International .338 Super Magnum (SM)
Caliber: .338 Lapua
Muzzle velocity: 3,000ft/sec (914 m/sec)
Weight: 15lb (6.8kg)
Barrel: 27.0 inches (686mm); four grooves, right-hand twist; one turn in 12 inches (305mm)
Magazine: Four rounds

United Kingdom: Accuracy International AW50

The AW50 was the company's move into the larger-caliber rifle market, and it has developed a most successful weapon, which has already seen active operational use in both Afghanistan and Iraq, where it has earned a very good reputation. It is chambered for the .50BMG round and weighs 33lb in its standard form and 28lb in a modified version with some titanium parts to reduce the

ABOVE: French Army Major Lombardini tries out a U.S. Marines Barrett "Light Fifty." The Barrett has been progressively modified over several years and is available in many versions. It continues to serve the military very well.

weight. It has a fluted barrel to increase cooling, and this is fitted with a particularly efficient muzzle brake. This, together with the bipod and soft-recoil system, make it a comfortable weapon to fire.

Data
Model: AWM 50
Caliber: .50BMG
Muzzle velocity: n.k.
Weight: 33lb (15.0 kg)
Barrel: 27.0 inches (686mm); four grooves, right-hand twist; one turn in 15 inches (305mm)
Magazine: Five rounds

United States: Barrett M82A1 "Light Fifty"

One of the first of the modern range of anti-materiel rifles firing the 0.50BMG round, the Barrett M82 first appeared in 1982 (hence the number in the designation), with the first orders being placed by Sweden in 1989 and by U.S. forces at the time of the first Gulf War. This rifle has undergone several version changes and upgrades over the past few years to keep it up to speed with other newer rifle designs now available. It is primarily used for anti-materiel work, where radars, aircraft, armored vehicles, or missile systems are the primary targets and not their operators. The rifle is easy to use and comfortable to fire, and can be mounted on vehicles or helicopters. There is considerable competition in this field, but the Barrett "Light Fifty" is still right up there with its rivals.

ABOVE: An early version of the M82 Barrett anti-materiel rifle in USMC service. Benefiting from progressive upgrades, it is used by armies throughout the world, and has been used at very short range by IRA terrorists against soldiers and police officers.

BELOW: The old M40A1 Remington sniper rifle has also now been updated with a newer McMillan stock, bipod, and Schmitt & Bender 3 x 12 variable telescopic sight. This original A1 is fitted with the Simrad "piggy-back" style night vision optic.

Data
Model: Barrett M82A1 Light Fifty
Caliber: .50inBMG (12.7 x 99mm)
Muzzle velocity: 2,788ft/sec (850m/sec)
Weight: 28.4lb (12.9kg)
Barrel: 29.0 inches (737mm)
Magazine: Ten rounds

United States: McMillan M93

McMillan has a very strong pedigree in the heavy rifle market and has had rifles operational for some time, the latest to be fielded being the M93, which is, in fact, an up-scaled M86 sniper rifle. The M93 has individual adjustment features to allow for different firers, a multi-hole muzzle-brake, and a folding stock for ease of transport and storage. The rifle has the same high standard and performance associated with all their other products and has been a military success around the world.

Data
Model: McMillan M93
Caliber: .50 x 99mm BMG
Muzzle velocity: 2,789ft/sec (850m/sec)
Weight: 21.5lb (9.75kg)
Barrel: 29.0 inches (737mm)
Magazine: Five rounds

United States: Marine Corps M40A1 Product Improved (PIP)

The U.S. Marines' weapon-manufacturing facility at Quantico, Virginia, took the basic M40 (Remington 700) and devised a series of modifications in order to produce a very accurate sniper weapon. The outcome was more like a completely new weapon than a modification and gave the marines a hand-made weapon with a totally redesigned McMillan fiberglass stock, complete with adjustable cheek piece, and an overall more ergonomic design. As with all current marine weapons, the M40A1PIP has seen considerable operational experience over the last few years and continues to give the marine sniper a first class weapon platform.

Data
Model: M40A1(PIP)
Caliber: 7.62 x 51mm
Muzzle velocity: 2,550ft/sec (777m/sec)
Weight: 14.5lb (6.58kg)
Barrel: 24.0 inches (610mm); four grooves; right-hand twist; one turn in 10 inches (254mm).
Magazine: Five rounds

United States: Marine Corps DMR (Designated Marksman Rifle) M14

The U.S. Marine Corps took the vast stock of older M14 rifles and modified some of them to produce a marksman rifle. It is a semi-automatic, gas-operated, magazine-fed weapon chambered for the standard NATO 7.62mm round. It has a fixed x10 scope, fiberglass stock, stainless steel barrel, and a detachable bipod. It is used by the observer in the U.S. Marines sniper team—the designated marksman—and also by the Fleet Anti-terrorist Support Team (FAST) companies of the Marine Corps Security Force Battalion, the Special Reaction Teams (SRT) of the Marine Corps Security Battalions, and the Explosive Ordnance Disposal (EOD) personnel, who use it for stand-off destruction of air-dropped munitions.

Data

Model: U.S. Marine Corps Designated Marksman Rifle (DMR)
Caliber: 7.62 x 51mm NATO
Muzzle velocity: 2,800ft/sec (853m/sec)
Weight: 11lb (5kg)
Barrel: 22.0 inches (559mm); right-hand twist; one turn in 12 inches (305mm)
Magazine: Twenty rounds

United States: Stoner SR25

Eugene Stoner is one of the most famous and respected rifle designers of all time and was responsible for the Armalite series and the M16, which are used by armed forces around the world. He was engaged by the Knight's Armament Company (KAC) to design a new sniper rifle and the outcome was the SR25, which, while sharing some characteristics of his earlier AR-10/M16 designs, is actually a totally new weapon designed specifically for the sniping role. The SR25 is considered by all users to be very accurate, but some have expressed reservations about its reliability in action.

Data

Model: Knight (Stoner) SR25
Caliber: 7.62 x 51mm NATO (.308in)
Muzzle velocity: 2,887ft/sec (880m/sec)
Weight: 10.75lb (4.88kg)
Barrel: 24.0 inches (609mm) (several variations exist); right-hand twist; one turn in 11.25 inches (285mm)
Magazine: Twenty-round box

RIGHT: The author tries out the M24 version of the Remington 700 series that is in service with the U.S. Army. The rifle is as reliable as any Remington, and serves its snipers well.

INDEX